30 day Breakthrough

PRAYER

Defeating Warfare

WRITTEN BY LILLIE M. FLOWERS

This book is dedicated to Angelic Furch

April 26, 1992 - June 3, 2022

30-day Breakthrough Prayer

Introduction

30-Day Breakthrough Prayer is designed for individuals who have encountered intense spiritual challenges involving unseen forces. Spiritual warfare can manifest in various forms, including interpersonal relationships, addictions, oppression, and internal struggles. This book provides practical guidance on prayer, detailing how to identify obstacles, surrender petitions to God, and deepen understanding of relevant scriptures incorporated into each prayer. The prayers are structured to dismantle strongholds and employ scripture as a protective tool, counteracting negative influences and affirming faith in Jesus Christ as defender. When adversity arises, this book emphasizes that believers can rely on God's sovereignty, equipping them to confront challenges using scriptural truth. The aim is to offer readers meaningful insights for spiritual growth and empowerment. For those already established in their faith, 30-Day Breakthrough Prayer serves as an excellent gift for individuals seeking support in their spiritual journey. It addresses common misconceptions about prayer, emphasizing that God desires a personal relationship with each individual.

30-day Breakthrough Prayer

Table of Contents

30-day Breakthrough Prayer

Chapter 1
Intercession

Heavenly Father, whom art in Heaven, hallow will be thy name. Allow this spiritual intercession into the assembly of heaven, allow these words written in prayer to bring harvest; that the reader shall ask of you, with great expectancy to receive, will seek your face, will find truth, hope, faith and perseverance. This petition is the intercession for their breakthrough, that you will hear their needs will be addressed answer these petition and break barriers and bondage thus that have kept them bound. Bless this journey of new beginnings into the understanding that with you nothing is impossible. We know that if we trust in you with our heart, lean not on our own understanding, you will direct us. For you say in your word, Jeremiah 29:11 "For I know the plans I have for you," declares the Lord, "plans to prosper you and not to harm you, plans to give you hope and a future." Now Lord, let this prayer open up the gates that you will hear from your people and begin guiding them a fresh beginning. Let the reader speak their needs int existence according to Matthew 21:22 "And all things, whatsoever ye shall ask in prayer, believing, ye shall receive."

Amen.

Chapter 2
Renewal

On this day, as every day, I will be renewed by the renewing of my mind. Each day I am renewed. My thoughts are above and not beneath. I will be in authority of my cognition to cast down my thoughts that are not of you, nor allowing my mental to be consumed by any destructive thoughts that would engage me into false beliefs or stagnate my purpose. According to 2 Corinthians 10:5 "Casting down imaginations, and every high thing that exalteth itself against the knowledge of God, and bringing into captivity every thought to the obedience of Christ", I realize my mind must be to the pulling down of strongholds in alignment to not think of what is passed away, but what is new and current, and pray about what is to come. In this dedication to my renewal, I am restored. Create in me a clean heart and renew an upright spirit into my soul, as referred to in your book of Psalms 51. Renew my alignment into new heights and new levels of thinking, new realms of understanding so that I am sharpened and acute. Renew my spirit of love in that I have compassion and the abilities of a sound mind. Renew my faith that I stand firm in all things that I hope for, expecting that it will come to pass. My renewal is also my rededication to you Lord Jesus, that I am made whole by my faith. I trust in your word, and I claim my victory over defeat. Right now, I am renewed into greater and not less, I am developing, and I continue to abound and gain further insight, strength, health, wealth, spiritual growth and magnitude of all things possible. In Jesus name.

Amen.

30-day Breakthrough Prayer

This prayer provides an exhaustive analysis and summary of the "Renewal" section within the "30-day Breakthrough Prayer." The core purpose of this text is to articulate a profound, daily commitment to spiritual and mental transformation, establishing a covenant of continuous renewal centered on aligning one's thoughts, spirit, and faith with divine principles. It serves as a declaration of authority over the mind, a petition for internal restoration mirroring biblical mandates, and an affirmation of expected victory and holistic abundance. The prayer emphasizes that breakthrough is not a singular event but the sustained result of actively managing one's cognition, rejecting stagnation, and embracing an ever-advancing state of spiritual and personal development.

The Daily Mandate of Mental Renewal

This section details the foundational commitment to continuous cognitive transformation, establishing renewal as a perpetual, daily occurrence rather than an occasional event.

- The declaration begins with the assertion that renewal is not conditional but an established reality: "On this day, as on every day, I will be renewed by the renewing of my mind." This establishes a proactive stance, ensuring that each new day begins with the expectation and acceptance of mental refreshment and revitalization.
- The scope of this renewal is defined by its orientation: "My thoughts are of above and not beneath." This establishes a clear vertical alignment, prioritizing heavenly perspectives, divine truths, and eternal values over earthly concerns.
- The commitment necessitates active stewardship over one's cognitive faculties, asserting immediate authority over the mind.
- This stewardship involves the conscious decision to govern cognition, ensuring that mental energy

is directed toward constructive, faith-based pathways rather than being passively surrendered to external or internal pressures.

- Destructive thoughts are identified as those that actively engage the individual in the acceptance of "false beliefs," which serve to undermine foundational truths and spiritual realities.
- Furthermore, the prayer recognizes that unchecked negative cognition has the power to "stagnate my purpose," halting forward momentum and preventing the fulfillment of divine assignments or personal destiny.
- Therefore, the daily renewal is a protective measure, a spiritual discipline designed to keep the mind sharp, focused, and aligned with the higher calling, preventing the erosion of purpose through mental compromise.
- This continuous process ensures that the individual remains actively engaged in the work of transformation, making the renewal of the mind the bedrock upon which all other breakthroughs are built and sustained throughout the thirty-day period and beyond.

Authority Over Cognition and Casting Down Strongholds (2 Corinthians 10:5)

This theme focuses on the active spiritual warfare required to maintain mental renewal, drawing directly from scripture to define the methodology for achieving cognitive freedom.

- The prayer invokes the powerful directive found in 2 Corinthians 10:5: "Casting down imaginations, and every high thing that exalteth itself against the knowledge of God and bringing into captivity every thought to the obedience of Christ." This scripture forms the operational manual for mental governance.
- The concept of "casting down imaginations" implies a deliberate and forceful rejection of mental constructs, scenarios, or narratives that do not align with truth.

- The focus extends to dismantling "every high thing that exalteth itself," which refers to any proud, arrogant, or self-elevating thought pattern that attempts to establish itself as superior to the established, authoritative knowledge of God.
- The goal of this cognitive dismantling is the successful "bringing into captivity every thought to the obedience of Christ."
- The realization inherent in this declaration is that the mind must be actively engaged in the "pulling down of strongholds." Strongholds are deeply entrenched patterns of negative thinking, deeply rooted false beliefs, or habitual mental traps that resist easy removal.
- Instead, the renewed mind must concentrate on "what is new and current," embracing present realities of grace, provision, and power available in the now.
- Furthermore, the renewed mind must engage proactively in intercession, learning to "pray about what is to come," thereby shaping the future through aligned thought and prayer rather than being passively subjected to unforeseen circumstances.
- This active spiritual engagement ensures that the mind becomes a tool for creation and alignment, rather than a repository for past failures or future anxieties.

Restoration and Spiritual Rebirth (Psalm 51)

The prayer transitions from warfare to restoration, petitioning for a deep, internal cleansing and the re-establishment of spiritual integrity.

- "I am restored." This is a declaration of wholeness achieved through the process of repentance and dedication.
- Psalm 51: "Create in me a clean heart." This asks for the very core of one's being, the seat of intention and motivation, to be made pure and undefiled.

- "Renew an upright spirit into my soul." This seeks the restoration of integrity, moral rectitude, and a spirit that is properly oriented toward God.
- This internal renewal is essential because the soul is the deep reservoir of our being; renewing the spirit within the soul ensures that the transformation is not merely superficial but deeply rooted and enduring.
- The prayer acknowledges that this restoration is foundational, setting the stage for higher levels of spiritual experience and understanding.
- This dedication is presented as a holistic act where the individual, through faith, receives complete restoration, moving from a state of brokenness or compromise back into a state of divine design and functionality.

Alignment, Understanding, and Renewed Affections

This section focuses on elevating the individual's perspective and emotional capacity through divine restructuring.

- The request is for a significant upgrade in mental and spiritual positioning: "Renew my alignment into new heights and new levels of thinking." This implies moving beyond previous ceilings of understanding and perspective.
- This elevation is further defined as entering "new realms of understanding," suggesting that the renewal grants access to previously inaccessible spiritual truths or insights.
- The practical outcome of this new alignment and understanding is clarity and precision: the individual desires to be "sharpened and acute," capable of discerning truth accurately and responding with focused intention.
- The renewal extends beyond intellect to the affective domain, specifically requesting the renewal of the "spirit of love."

- This renewed spirit of love is directly linked to practical virtues: it fosters "compassion" for others and grants the "abilities of a sound mind."
- A sound mind is characterized by balance, wisdom, and the capacity to make judgments free from the influence of fear, confusion, or destructive imaginations previously mentioned to be destroyed for removal in the reset.
- The renewal process thus creates a comprehensive transformation: higher thought, deeper understanding, focused acuity, and a foundation of divine love enabling practical wisdom and empathy.

The Renewal of Faith and Trust in the Word

A critical component of the breakthrough prayer is the reinforcement of belief and unwavering reliance on divine promises, ensuring stability amidst ongoing transformation.

- "Renew my faith that I stand firm in all things that I hope for." This is actively "expect that it will come to pass." This moves faith from passive belief to active anticipation of fulfillment.
- The entire process "My renewal is also my rededication to you Lord Jesus." This underscores that the transformation is relational, directed toward deepening the covenant with Christ.
- The desired result of this rededication is complete integration and healing: "that I am made whole by my faith." Wholeness encompasses spiritual, mental, and perhaps even physical aspects, all grounded by belief.

Claiming Victory and Manifesting Abundance

- "Right now, I am renewed into greater and not less."
- The individual acknowledges an ongoing process of development: "I am developing." This recognizes that spiritual maturity requires continuous effort.

30-day Breakthrough Prayer

The "Renewal" prayer is a powerful blueprint for sustained spiritual breakthrough achieved primarily through rigorous mental discipline and unwavering faith. The key takeaway is that transformation is an active, daily endeavor requiring the individual to assert authority over their cognition, dismantling negative thought patterns and strongholds by aligning every thought with the obedience of Christ, as mandated by scripture.

30-day Breakthrough Prayer

Chapter 3

Love is Perfected in Jesus Christ

Lord, I've come to accept that your love is perfect, and perfected as the greatest love. I've searched love, I've loved and I've lost love, until I came to where you are, I can work to perfect love but only less I engage love in your likeness. Bitter moments did I allow to cipher through my heart, and I slowly became enraged at love rewards.

Is it true that love is punishing or is it that love is imperfect unless it is the Agape of measure through the love that you have explained, taught and demonstrated. In my instruction I was told that before the father, you would appear before me, so that God would see his Son, the reflection of himself and not of my bitter heart. Or is it that If I ask in your name that you fix me, and you shall erase all bitterness of a tarnished heart into the perfection of goodness and grace which I am nothing like?

I look to you as my teacher, for your ancient is from the beginning. Teach me of the wisdom that gives root and seed to salvation. If it be a narrow road, lead me along the way. Let me not get weary and faint. The trying of this journey has tested me, and my path was not straight, nor easy, nor pleasant but pain enduring. I too, rejected but not as a cornerstone but a simple man.

Little understanding comes from dreadful obnoxious madness, ignorance nor a massacre but yet, mares of the night surprises us and yet you love and forgive and overcame the world, knowing that the very ones you gave your life for was who'd you would die for. Greatest love of all is what you accomplished.

30-day Breakthrough Prayer

Prayer

Lord Jesus, help me to love spiritually by seeing you in others as God sees you in me. Knead me understanding so that I can understand that many of us fall short and that love doesn't come from the world, but from above, and this perfect love must be sought and appreciated as a gift, because you gave your life as an offering to bring eternal life to death thereby bringing eternal life to life. Thank you Jesus for your love.

The Profound Journey Toward Perfected Love in Christ

This prayer presents a deeply personal and theological reflection on the nature of divine love, centered on the assertion that "Love is perfected in Jesus Christ." It functions as an extended meditation, moving from an acknowledgment of personal failings in the search for love to a fervent prayer for spiritual transformation. The text explores the contrast between worldly, imperfect love and the ultimate standard of Agape. The core purpose is to articulate a desire to shed personal bitterness and embrace a divinely bestowed, perfect love that enables one to see Christ reflected in others and appreciate the gift of eternal life.

The Acceptance of Perfect Love

The foundational theme of this reflection is the necessary acceptance of divine love as the ultimate standard, a concept that requires profound personal surrender.

- Acknowledging Perfection: The love experienced through Christ is inherently perfect and stands as the greatest form of love attainable. The journey described involves actively searching for love, experiencing the pain of loving and subsequently losing love, indicating a history rooted in temporal attachments that inevitably fail to satisfy the soul's deepest longings. The arrival at this realization—"until I came to where you are"—is presented not as a passive discovery but as a destination reached through trial and error in the pursuit of lesser loves.

- The Limitation of Self-Effort: The text immediately qualifies the ability to manifest this perfect love, noting that personal efforts to achieve perfection are inherently limited unless they are actively engaged "in your likeness." This implies that human attempts at perfecting love are insufficient on their own; they require divine modeling and infusion. The struggle against personal flaws is evident in the admission of allowing "Bitter moments" to infiltrate the heart. These moments are described as a process of internal ciphering, suggesting a slow, corrosive breakdown of spirit. This internal corrosion leads to a negative emotional state: becoming "slowly became enraged at love rewards." This suggests that when earthly or self-centered expectations of love are not met, the individual turns hostile or resentful toward the very concept of reward or fulfillment derived from love, highlighting a deep spiritual misalignment.
- The Need for Divine Engagement: To move past this internal rage and stagnation, the author recognizes the necessity of actively engaging with love as demonstrated by Christ. This engagement is not merely intellectual assent but a practical, lived commitment to mirroring the divine pattern, suggesting that perfection is achieved through imitation and participation in the divine nature of love.

Distinguishing Agape from Imperfect Experience

A central theological inquiry within the text revolves around defining the true nature of love, specifically contrasting punitive or flawed experiences with the concept of Agape.

- Questioning the Nature of Love: The reflection poses a critical dichotomy: Is love inherently punishing, or is it only imperfect when it fails to meet the standard of Agape? This question probes the common human experience where love often feels difficult, demanding, or even painful.
- The Desire for Divine Reflection: The author expresses a profound yearning for a complete internal transformation, contrasting the desired state with the current "bitter heart." The instruction received suggests a future state where before the Father, the individual will appear as the reflection of the Son, not as the embodiment of personal bitterness. This highlights the theological concept of justification and sanctification, where the believer is seen through Christ's perfection. The prayerful request is explicit: to erase all bitterness from a "tarnished heart" and replace it with the "perfection of goodness and grace." This transformation is framed as something utterly beyond the author's inherent capability ("which I am nothing like?"), emphasizing reliance on divine intervention for true moral and spiritual refinement.

Seeking Ancient Wisdom on the Path of Faith

The text shifts focus to the role of Jesus as the ultimate source of knowledge and guidance necessary to navigate the challenges inherent in pursuing this perfect love.

- The Teacher of Antiquity: The author looks to Jesus as the teacher whose wisdom is foundational, noting that His origin or "ancient is from the beginning." This establishes the timeless, eternal authority of the wisdom being sought. The specific wisdom requested is that which "gives root and seed to salvation." This is not merely abstract knowledge but practical, life-giving instruction that establishes a firm foundation for eternal life.

- Commitment to the Narrow Road: The acceptance of the path ahead is characterized by realism regarding its difficulty. If the way is decreed to be "a narrow road," the plea is simply for divine assistance to remain on it, specifically asking not to "get weary and faint." The path has proven to be anything but "straight, nor easy, nor pleasant," emphasizing endurance through pain ("pain enduring"). This validates the struggles faced by the believer as part of the intended process of refinement.
- Shared Experience of Rejection: The author draws a parallel between the divine experience and personal suffering, stating, "I too, rejected but not as a cornerstone but a simple man." This line powerfully contrasts the author's rejection—that of an ordinary, perhaps insignificant individual—with the ultimate rejection faced by Christ, who was rejected yet became the essential cornerstone of faith. This comparison serves to contextualize personal suffering within the grand narrative of divine suffering and ultimate triumph.

Triumph Over Darkness and Ignorance

The reflection addresses the overwhelming nature of worldly troubles and the power of divine love to supersede them, even when understanding seems elusive.

- The Limits of Human Comprehension: True understanding is positioned as something that does not arise from negative, chaotic human experiences such as "dreadful obnoxious madness, ignorance nor a massacre." These elements represent the depths of worldly despair and confusion. Despite these overwhelming forces, the text asserts the persistent nature of divine love: "yet, mares of the night surprises us and yet you love and forgive and overcame the world." This emphasizes that divine action is constant, even when the believer is caught unaware or overwhelmed by sudden darkness ("mares of the night").

- The Paradox of Sacrifice: The ultimate demonstration of this conquering love is rooted in the sacrificial act directed toward those who were the object of that sacrifice. The profound realization is that Christ gave His life specifically for "the very ones you gave your life for was who'd you would die for." This highlights the radical, counter-intuitive nature of Christian love—dying for those who are inherently flawed or even hostile.
- The Accomplishment of Greatest Love: The culmination of this sacrificial act is defined as the "Greatest love of all is what you accomplished." This shifts the focus from the act itself to the completed result—the victory over sin, death, and the world achieved through the cross and resurrection. This accomplishment is the bedrock upon which the believer's hope for transformation rests.

The Concluding Supplication for Spiritual Sight and Gratitude

The prayer concludes with a direct prayer, synthesizing the preceding reflections into actionable requests for spiritual growth and appreciation.

- The Prayer for Spiritual Sight: The central petition is for the ability to "love spiritually by seeing you in others as God sees you in me." It requires a shift in perception, moving beyond superficial judgment to viewing others through the lens of divine acceptance and potential, mirroring the grace received by the supplicant.
- Kneading for Understanding: The request to be "Knead[ed] understanding" suggests a deep, almost physical reshaping of the mind and spirit to grasp fundamental truths about human failing and divine provision. The specific understanding sought is the recognition that "many of us fall

short," acknowledging universal human imperfection. Crucially, this understanding must encompass the origin of true love: it "doesn't come from the world, but from above." This reinforces the distinction between temporal affection and eternal Agape.

- Appreciating the Gift: Because perfect love originates from above, it must be actively "sought and appreciated as a gift." It is not earned through the struggles detailed in the earlier sections but received freely. This appreciation is directly tied to the ultimate sacrifice: "because you gave your life as an offering to bring eternal life to life." The gift of love is inseparable from the gift of eternal life secured by Christ's offering.
- Final Thanksgiving: The prayer concludes with simple gratitude: "Thank you Jesus for your love." This final expression solidifies the document's trajectory—from struggle and questioning to acceptance, understanding, and heartfelt thanks for the perfected love that makes transformation possible.

The prayer serves as a profound testament to the transformative power inherent in accepting Jesus Christ as the source of perfect love. Key takeaways emphasize that personal attempts to achieve perfect love are insufficient, often leading to bitterness when earthly expectations fail. True spiritual progress requires seeking the ancient wisdom that guides one through a difficult, testing journey. The core message is that divine Agape transcends worldly chaos, ignorance, and suffering, culminating in the ultimate accomplishment of Christ's sacrifice. The final aspiration is practical: to cultivate spiritual sight, enabling the believer to see Christ in others, recognize love as a divine gift rather than an earned reward, and live in perpetual gratitude for the eternal life secured by that perfect love. The entire text is an earnest plea for the grace necessary to move from a tarnished heart to one

30-day Breakthrough Prayer

reflecting the goodness and grace achieved only through Christ

30-day Breakthrough Prayer

Chapter 4

Morning Glory

Hallelujah! Morning Glory, shine your light on us - Happy Day.

Give us a joyous spirit, let us be excited for the frequency of joy.

Let All those of good cheer, join in and celebrate the day that the Lord has made.

Each day is a gift, and I give you thanks for your wonders and your boundless magnitude.

I pray that the spirit of calm and peace be my companion as I ask the Lord for sound judgment in every situation.

Let your greatness be upon us, and the strength of endurance and wisdom keep yielding creativity and let us work for the greater of what is good and rewarding.

Let purpose hold its place as the winning award of who, what, when, where and why I am here perfected in time and order according to your will.

Welcome patience into my dwelling that I am not anxious in activity, response, reply or reaction.

Stretch forth your hand to your people and provide us with bounty the needs and necessity where there will be no lack - provide us into the intake of overflow.

Prepare my mental with the newness of the day and that I shall not entertain the temptation nor moments of past time.

Give us this day, our daily bread, and I will give you thanks for all things you provide.

In each day there is thanksgiving, you are worthy to be praised, in Jesus name.

Amen.

30-day Breakthrough Prayer

Morning Glory: A Comprehensive Exegesis of Daily Affirmation

This prayer provides an exhaustive summary and expansion of the devotional text titled "Morning Glory." The source material is a concise, yet profound, prayer or affirmation intended to set a spiritual and mental tone for the day. It functions as a comprehensive petition covering aspects of spiritual awakening, the cultivation of positive inner character traits, the request for divine guidance and purpose, the assurance of material and spiritual provision, and the commitment to perpetual gratitude.

The Invocation of Light and Joyful Expectation

This initial theme centers on the direct address to the "Morning Glory," asking for illumination and the establishment of a positive emotional baseline for the day ahead.

- The Call for Illumination: The opening declaration, "Hallelujah! Morning Glory, shine your light on us - Happy Day," serves as an immediate recognition of divine presence as the source of all positive energy. This light is not merely physical but represents clarity, truth, and the dispelling of confusion or darkness that might obscure the path forward. The request is for this divine radiance to permeate the individual's entire being, setting the stage for a day characterized by happiness.

- Cultivating a Spirit of Joy: The text explicitly requests, "Give us a joyous spirit, let us be excited for the frequency of joy." This moves beyond passive hope; it is an active solicitation for an internal disposition—a joyous spirit—that is ready and eager to perceive and engage with positive occurrences. Excitement for the "frequency of joy" implies an expectation that joy will not be a singular event but a recurring pattern throughout the day, contingent upon maintaining the requested internal state.
- Communal Celebration: The affirmation extends outward: "Let All those of Good cheer, join in and celebrate the day that the Lord has made." This emphasizes the communal aspect of faith and happiness. The day is recognized as a divine creation, making celebration mandatory. It calls for the alignment of one's own cheer with that of others who share a similar positive outlook, reinforcing the idea that spiritual well-being is both personal and relational.
- Acknowledging the Gift of Time: The recognition that "Each day is a gift, and I give you thanks for your wonder and your boundless magnitude" anchors the celebration in profound gratitude. Every twenty-four hours is framed not as an obligation but as a precious, unearned endowment. This perspective shifts the focus from daily demands to the inherent miraculous nature of existence, acknowledging the vastness and complexity ("boundless magnitude") of the creator's works, which are manifested even in the mundane structure of a new day. The Pursuit of Inner Tranquility and Spiritual Companionship

This section focuses on securing internal stability, particularly in the face of potential stress or uncertainty inherent in daily decision-making.

- The Prayer for Calm and Peace: A central petition is the request for "the spirit of calm and peace be my companion." This elevates calm and peace from temporary states to constant companions, suggesting a desired state of being rather than a fleeting emotion.

- Seeking Sound Judgment: The companion of calm is requested precisely when the individual "ask[s] the Lord for sound judgment in every situation." This links emotional regulation directly to cognitive function. True judgment, the text implies, cannot be achieved under duress or anxiety; it requires the steadying influence of peace. Sound judgment is thus presented as a divinely assisted faculty necessary for navigating complexity.
- The Foundation of Divine Presence: The request for greatness to be "upon us" sets the stage for the necessary mental fortitude. This is not a request for personal glory but for the overshadowing presence of the divine, which acts as a protective and empowering layer over the individual's actions and perceptions throughout the day.

The Request for Divine Attributes: Wisdom, Endurance, and Creativity

Moving beyond mere peace, this theme addresses the active tools required for productive and meaningful engagement with the world.

- Endurance as a Sustaining Force: The text asks that "the strength of endurance" be present. Endurance is crucial for navigating long-term goals and resisting the temptation to quit when challenges arise. It is the spiritual stamina required to see tasks through to completion, regardless of immediate feedback or difficulty.
- Wisdom Guiding Action: Together with endurance is the need for "wisdom." Wisdom here is not just knowledge, but the discerning ability to apply that knowledge correctly. This wisdom is specifically linked to a generative outcome: it must "keep yielding creativity."
- Creativity as a Productive Output: The concept of creativity is framed as a direct, positive

byproduct of endurance and wisdom. This creativity is channeled toward meaningful action: "let us work for the greater of what is good and rewarding." This establishes a clear ethical framework for productivity—work must serve a higher good and result in something genuinely beneficial, not merely self-serving or transient. The synergy between endurance, wisdom, and creativity ensures that effort is both sustained and effective in achieving positive moral outcomes.

Establishing Divine Order and Purposeful Existence

This section delves into the philosophical and existential grounding of the day, seeking clarity on one's role and timing within a larger divine plan.

- Purpose as the Ultimate Reward: The affirmation demands that "Let purpose hold its place as the winning award." This radically reorients ambition. The primary goal is not external success or material gain, but the successful realization and execution of one's inherent purpose. Purpose is positioned as the ultimate prize, surpassing all other accolades.
- Defining the Self Through Divine Context: The text seeks clarity on the fundamental questions of existence: "who, what, when, where why I am here." This is a comprehensive request for existential mapping. By seeking this clarity, the individual aims to understand their identity (who), their function (what), their timing (when), their location (where), and their motivation (why).
- Alignment with Divine Timing: Crucially, this understanding must be "perfected in time and order according to your will." This submission acknowledges that the individual's perceived purpose must align perfectly with a higher, predetermined schedule and structure. The perfection sought is not in the individual's execution alone, but in the flawless integration

of their actions into the divine timeline, ensuring that effort is never wasted against the flow of providence. Cultivating Patience and Managing Daily Reactions

This theme addresses the immediate, moment-to-moment interactions that define the quality of a day, focusing heavily on emotional regulation and responsiveness.

- Welcoming Patience: The invitation, "Welcome patience into my dwelling," personifies patience as a necessary resident. This welcome is active and intentional, suggesting that patience must be intentionally invited in, rather than passively waited for.
- The Avoidance of Reactive Anxiety: The purpose of welcoming patience is explicitly defined by what it prevents: "that I am not anxious in activity, response, reply or reaction." This highlights four critical areas where anxiety typically manifests: general activity (busyness), responding to external stimuli, formulating verbal replies, and immediate emotional reactions. The goal is to insert a thoughtful pause between stimulus and action across all these vectors.
- The Space for Deliberation: By cultivating patience, the individual creates necessary space. Anxiety leads to hurried, often regrettable, actions. Patience ensures that every interaction—whether physical activity, a verbal response, or an internal emotional reaction—is measured, deliberate, and aligned with the previously established goals of peace and sound judgment. This cultivation is essential for maintaining the integrity of the morning's spiritual commitments throughout the day's inevitable pressures.

Petition for Abundant Provision and Overflowing Supply

This section shifts focus to material and spiritual sustenance, moving beyond sufficiency to a state of abundance that benefits others.

- The Outstretched Hand of Provision: The prayer asks the divine to "Stretch forth your hand to your people and provide us with bounty the needs and necessity." This is a communal request for provision, recognizing that the individual is part of a larger body of "people." The provision covers both "needs" (essentials) and "necessity" (things required for the specific context of the day).
- Eliminating Lack: The desired outcome is absolute: "where there will be no lack." This is a powerful declaration of faith against scarcity, asserting that the divine supply is comprehensive enough to cover every legitimate requirement.
- The Mandate of Overflow: The provision is not meant to stop at sufficiency; it must lead to surplus: "provide us into the intake of overflow." This is perhaps the most generous aspect of the petition. The individual asks not just to be filled, but to be filled past the brim so that the excess can be distributed. This overflow is the mechanism by which the individual can fulfill their purpose of working "for the greater of what is good and rewarding," as it provides the resources—time, energy, material goods—to share with others. This transforms personal blessing into a conduit for communal benefit.

Mental Fortification Against Temptation and Past Regrets

This theme addresses the internal landscape of the mind, seeking protection from both future pitfalls and lingering historical burdens.

- Embracing Mental Newness: The request to "Prepare my mental with the newness of the day" is a conscious act of mental renewal. It demands a scrubbing clean of yesterday's clutter, anxieties, and unresolved issues, preparing the mind as a fresh slate ready to receive the day's specific challenges and opportunities.
- Rejecting Temptation: A critical element of this mental preparation is the resolve "that I shall not entertain the temptation." This is an active

refusal to engage with potential moral or spiritual pitfalls. By preparing the mind with newness, the individual builds a defense mechanism that rejects the initial lure of temptation before it can take root.

- Severing Ties with the Past: Equally important is the commitment "nor moments of past time." This addresses the psychological burden of regret, rumination, or dwelling on past failures or successes. The new day requires full mental presence; lingering in past moments—whether painful or nostalgic—diverts the energy needed for present action and future purpose. The mental preparation is thus dual: forward-looking clarity combined with a decisive release of historical baggage.

The Covenant of Daily Sustenance and Perpetual Thanksgiving

The final lines solidify the relationship between receiving provision and expressing gratitude, framing the entire day within a cycle of divine giving and human thanks.

- The Echo of Daily Bread: The invocation directly references the traditional prayer: "Give us this day, our daily bread." This anchors the modern, complex requests within a timeless, fundamental acknowledgment of dependence on a higher power for basic sustenance. It is a humble recognition that even with requests for overflow and wisdom, the foundation remains the simple, necessary provision for the current twenty-four hours.
- Reciprocal Gratitude: In response to receiving this bread and all other provisions, the speaker pledges, "and I will give you thanks for all things you provide." This establishes a clear covenant: receiving is inextricably linked to thanking. This gratitude is comprehensive, covering all things provided, suggesting an acceptance of both the easy blessings and the

difficult lessons that might also be considered "provisions."

- The Inherent State of Thanksgiving: The concluding thought reinforces this commitment: "In each day there is thanksgiving." This elevates thanksgiving from an action performed at the end of the day to an inherent quality of the day itself. If one is truly living in the light and purpose requested earlier, thanksgiving becomes the natural atmosphere breathed in and out.
- Final Declaration of Worthiness: The text culminates in the ultimate declaration of faith: "you are worthy to be praised, in Jesus' name. Amen." This final affirmation shifts the focus entirely away from the self and back to the divine, confirming that the entire preceding litany of requests is predicated on the absolute, unchanging worthiness of the recipient of the prayer. The "Amen" seals the commitment to live out the intentions set forth in the invocation.

The "Morning Glory" text outlines a comprehensive spiritual strategy for navigating daily existence. It functions as a holistic blueprint for intentional living, beginning with an energetic invocation of divine light and joy, immediately followed by a deep commitment to internal stability through peace and sound judgment. The prayer meticulously balances requests for active spiritual tools—endurance, wisdom, and creativity—with the need for existential grounding via clearly defined purpose aligned with divine will. Furthermore, it addresses the practical realities of life by petitioning for provision that leads to overflow, ensuring resources are available not just for the self but for the community. Crucially, the text demands rigorous mental discipline, requiring the active rejection of anxiety, temptation, and past regrets in favor of mental newness. Ultimately, the entire framework is sustained by a continuous cycle of recognizing daily sustenance and expressing unwavering, comprehensive thanksgiving. The key takeaway is that a "Happy Day" is achieved not by controlling external events, but by proactively aligning one's inner spirit, actions, and perspective with a divinely ordered reality, culminating in perpetual praise.

30-day Breakthrough Prayer

Chapter 5

Deliver Me

There is a great trouble within the habitat of a divination which is shelling skins of disdain. I pray away the wrath of a filthy place full of a hate which has cankered like an earth worm through the trees which bring ripeness of sweet fruit. I cry help and pray away the evil of reckoning. I look to the hills from which comes my help. Dry out the sickness, destroy the evil oh Lord, pull it like an old, decayed tooth straight away the canal digging roots until the rot is gone. Strengthen me.

They have drawn their bow and pointed arrows all around me, they cheer and chant of destruction at the innocent, they've taken the oath of evil against the children. They've robbed the homeless and keep the barnyard full for themselves. I cry mercy! Ooh Lord, open your ears and hear my cry to the heavens, look upon this place and use your wind and power with the force of righteousness. For you say in your word:

Psalms 91: 4 He will cover you with his feathers,
and under his wings you will find refuge; his
faithfulness will be your shield and rampart.
5 You will not fear the terror of night,
nor the arrow that flies by day,
6 nor the pestilence that stalks in the darkness,
nor the plague that destroys at midday.
7 A thousand may fall at your side,
ten thousand at your right hand,
but it will not come near you.
8 You will only observe with your eyes
and see the punishment of the wicked.

Save us from the torment and destruction they cause upon your people. Search my soul, scan my heart and see for yourself if there be anything you despise. My strength went weary from lifting myself to rise and defend myself, but their camp was many, they outnumbered me, surrounded me with animals to tear at my soul. They've used my children as scatter and placed cursing and laugh when our sons and daughter had breath no longer, it's their strength and greatness to taunt suffering. In your word Jeremiah 31:15, my tears are brought forth, and you heard me wail, "A voice was heard in Ramah, lamentation and bitter weeping; Rachel, weeping for her children, refused to be comforted for her children, because they were no more." Answer my petition, let this time be today that you answer saying **Jeremiah 31:3-6**:

"I have loved you with an everlasting love;
    I have drawn you with unfailing kindness.
4 I will build you up again,
    and you, Virgin Israel, will be rebuilt.
Again you will take up your timbrels
    and go out to dance with the joyful.
5 Again you will plant vineyards
    on the hills of Samaria;
the farmers will plant them
    and enjoy their fruit.
6 There will be a day when watchmen cry out
    on the hills of Ephraim,
'Come, let us go up to
  to the Lord our God.

Grief is yours; your mighty hand removed the lingering spirit of heaviness from my heart that your will be done.

Answer me with your voice, let me hear you speak as you did in **Jeremiah 31:16-17**

"Restrain your voice from weeping
    and your eyes from tears,
for your work will be rewarded,"
declares the Lord.
    "They will return from the land of the enemy.
17So there is hope for your descendants,"
declares the Lord.
    "Your children will return to their own land."

Lord, search upon my heart, hear my soul cry out for you. There was not a friend or mother to comfort me. They looked and it was their joy in all my suffering. These were who I knew and had offered my goodness and friendship to and they cut at my heart and in secret gave poison to my flesh that I should be sickened and die. I call your name Jehovah, you are power, you are my hope, you are my God. Keep my soul from torture, torment, mental anguish and disparity. Provide your restoration and bring the dry bones to life, awaken my spirit as you did with Lazarus, let me not die. In Jesus name, the Christ. Shalom.

Let my light never dim, fill my cup that my well never dry up, for my cup overflow, feed me with bread from the heavens, as you said in John 6:35:

> "And Jesus said unto them, I am the bread of life: he that cometh to me shall never hunger; and he that believeth on me shall never thirst"
>
> .

oh, my soul, bless my seed, I offer my children to be blessed as you bless those who are called by your name Jesus fills me with love, hope, strength, faith, I have called my children by your fruit and names of your prophets. I adore you; I ask that you bring faith in a double portion, give me vision and discernment and your words that I can speak of your kingdom and mighty name. Hallelujah! Peace and praise belong to you Lord Jesus, you've triumphed the world when you were slain with no stain or disdain.

They sowed their seeds with man-made seeds, not treasure from heaven but the things that parish away. They've given over to worship what parishes away. If you bring destruction, who can stand against you. I pray your mercy will save us from the frivolity of foolishness and evil men who have placed your people in chains, bondage and placed them in camps, stolen their children and scattered them into the streets, those who do evil deeds in the working of darkness. Send your angels of protection against the wars of destruction, to save your people. Praise and glory be to God for your throne is forever.

Amen.

A Devotional Plea for Deliverance, Restoration, and Divine Refuge

This document, titled "Deliver Me," is a profound and impassioned prayer or devotional text expressing deep spiritual anguish, betrayal, and an unwavering appeal to the Divine for immediate rescue and comprehensive restoration. The supplicant navigates a landscape of intense suffering, characterized by external oppression and internal decay, contrasting this tribulation with vivid recollections of scriptural promises of protection, particularly from the Psalms. The text moves through stages of lamentation, citing historical sorrows like Rachel's weeping, before culminating in declarations of faith in God's everlasting love, the redemptive power of Jesus Christ as the Bread of Life, and the ultimate triumph over forces of darkness and destruction. It is a comprehensive cry for salvation, spiritual sustenance, and the rebuilding of a scattered people.

The Initial Lament and Demand for Cleansing

- The prayer begins by establishing the severity of the current affliction, describing a "great trouble within the habitat of a divination," setting a tone of deep spiritual distress that permeates the environment.
- This trouble is characterized by a pervasive sense of disdain, metaphorically described as the Divine being "shelling skins of disdain," suggesting a stripping away of dignity or protection.

- The source of the pain is identified as a pervasive, corrupting force: the "wrath of a filthy place full of a hate which has cankered like an earth worm," indicating a deep, insidious rot spreading through what should be sources of life and goodness.
- This corruption is shown to affect even the natural order, as the hate has spread "through the trees which bring ripeness of sweet fruit," symbolizing how evil taints potential joy and productivity.
- The supplicant actively seeks to counteract this spiritual poison by crying out to "pray away the evil of reckoning," acknowledging the need for divine intervention to stop the cycle of judgment or consequence.
- In seeking a solution, the focus shifts upward, recognizing the sole source of aid: "I look to the hills from which comes my help," a classic biblical reference to divine assistance.
- The plea for healing is aggressive and thorough, demanding that the sickness be eradicated completely, asking the Lord to "Dry out the sickness, destroy the evil."
- A particularly visceral image is used to convey the necessity of complete removal: the evil must be pulled out "like an old decaying tooth straight away the canal digging roots until the rot is gone," emphasizing that superficial fixes are insufficient; the root cause must be eliminated.
- The foundational request for personal empowerment follows this plea for cleansing: "Strengthen me," recognizing that the battle requires divine reinforcement.

The Siege of Enemies and Invocation of Psalm 91

- The immediate danger is depicted as an active military threat, with enemies having "drawn their bow and pointed arrows all around me," signifying constant, targeted aggression.

- These adversaries are not merely acting in silence; they actively celebrate the suffering, as they "cheer and chant of destruction at the innocent."
- The text details specific acts of injustice committed by these oppressors, noting that they have "taken the oath of evil against the children."
- Furthermore, their greed is highlighted through material theft: they have "robbed the homeless and keep the barnyard full for themselves," illustrating a profound imbalance of provision and cruelty.
- Overwhelmed by this injustice, the supplicant cries out in desperation: "I cry mercy! Ooh Lord, open your ears and hear my cry to the heavens."
- This cry is coupled with an appeal for a visible manifestation of divine power: to "look upon this place and use your wind and power with the force of righteousness."
- The basis for this expectation is rooted firmly in scripture, specifically citing Psalms 91:4, which serves as the covenantal guarantee of safety.
- The promise of divine shelter is detailed: the Lord "will cover you with his feathers," and under His wings, refuge will be found, with His faithfulness acting as an impenetrable "shield and rampart."
- This divine covering negates specific sources of fear, assuring protection from the "terror of night" and the "arrow that flies by day."
- The protection extends to unseen threats as well, guarding against "the pestilence that stalks in the darkness" and the "plague that destroys at midday."
- The magnitude of this protection is emphasized by the sheer scale of potential disaster that will be averted: even if "A thousand may fall at your side, ten thousand at your right hand," the individual under God's care "will not come near you."
- The outcome of this divine intervention is passive observation of justice: the protected will "only

observe with your eyes and see the punishment of the wicked."

Personal Anguish, Betrayal, and Historical Echoes

- The prayer shifts to a direct appeal for rescue from the immediate consequences of the conflict: "Save us from the torment and destruction they cause upon your people."
- A profound act of self-examination is requested, asking the Lord to "Search my soul, scan my heart and see for yourself if there be anything you despise," seeking purity as a prerequisite for deliverance.
- The physical and spiritual toll of resistance is acknowledged, noting that the supplicant's "strength went weary from lifting myself to rise up and defend myself."
- The overwhelming nature of the opposition is reiterated: "their camp was many, they outnumbered me."
- The assault is described as multifaceted, involving spiritual attacks symbolized by being "surrounded me with animals to tear at my soul."
- A deep sense of betrayal surfaces, as those who were once trusted have turned hostile, using the children as instruments of scattering.
- The cruelty of the oppressors is highlighted by their reaction to loss: they "laughed when the daughter you gave me had breath no longer," deriving satisfaction from mocking the suffering endured.
- The depth of this sorrow prompts a reference to historical weeping, citing Jeremiah 31:15, where the speaker's tears were brought forth and God heard the wail.
- The text vividly recalls the scene of Rachel in Ramah, "weeping for her children, refused to be comforted for her children, because they were no more," linking the current suffering to a foundational national tragedy.

- This historical context fuels an urgent demand for immediate divine action: "Answer my petition, let this time be today that you answer."

The Divine Response: Everlasting Love and Rebuilding

- The anticipated answer from the Lord is quoted, beginning with the assurance of eternal affection: "I have loved you with an everlasting love."
- This love is demonstrated through action, as the people have been drawn "with unfailing kindness."
- The promise of reconstruction is central to this divine response: "I will build you up again."
- This rebuilding is specifically directed toward the identity of the people: "and you, Virgin Israel, will be rebuilt."
- The restoration is intrinsically linked to future joy and celebration, promising that the people "Again you will take up your timbrels and go out to dance with the joyful."
- Agricultural prosperity returns as a sign of peace, indicating that they "Again you will plant vineyards on the hills of Samaria," and the farmers will finally "enjoy their fruit."
- A future day of communal calling is prophesied, where watchmen on the hills of Ephraim will cry out, inviting others: "Come, let us go up to Zion, to the Lord our God.'"
- The text acknowledges the transition from sorrow to peace, noting that "Grief is yours," but that the Lord's "mighty hand removed the lingering spirit of heaviness from my heart," ensuring that His divine will is accomplished.

Assurance of Reward and Return from Exile

- The Lord continues to speak, offering direct commands to cease the outward signs of mourning: "Restrain your voice from weeping and your eyes from tears."

- The reason provided for this cessation of grief is the certainty of divine recompense: "for your work will be rewarded," declares the Lord.
- The promise of repatriation is absolute: "They will return from the land of the enemy."
- This future promise solidifies hope for succeeding generations: "So there is hope for your descendants," declares the Lord.
- The final confirmation of this return is stated clearly: "Your children will return to their own land."

Deep Personal Petition and Identification with Christ

- The supplicant renews the plea for intimate spiritual inspection: "See Lord, search upon my heart, hear my soul cry out for you."
- The isolation experienced is emphasized again, noting the lack of comfort from "a friend or mother."
- The pain of betrayal is revisited, describing how those trusted looked upon the suffering with joy, secretly administering "poison to my flesh that I should be sickened and die."
- In this moment of deepest vulnerability, the supplicant calls upon the powerful name of God: "I call your name Jehovah, you are power, you are my hope, you are my God."
- The prayer focuses on preserving the inner self from ongoing harm: a request to "Keep my soul from torture, torment, mental anguish and disparity."
- A miraculous revival is sought, asking for "restoration" and the animation of the "dry bones to life," specifically requesting the spirit be awakened "as you did with Lazarus, let me not die."
- This desperate plea is sealed by invoking the authority of the Messiah: "In Jesus name, the Christ. Shalom."
- The petition then turns to the theme of unending spiritual provision, asking that the inner light

"never dim" and the spiritual cup "never dry up," leading to an overflow.

- This need for divine sustenance is explicitly linked to Christ's teaching, referencing John 6:35: the need to be fed "with bread from the heavens."
- The text quotes Jesus' declaration in full: "And Jesus said unto them, I am the bread of life: he that cometh to me shall never hunger; and he that believeth on me shall never thirst."

Final Dedication, Confrontation of Evil, and Eternal Praise

- The prayer extends blessings outward, asking that the supplicant's "seed" and children be blessed, mirroring those called by the name of Jesus.
- The internal state desired is a filling with divine attributes: "fill me with love, hope, strength, faith."
- The children have been dedicated by being named after the "fruit and names of your prophets."
- The supplicant expresses adoration and requests specific spiritual endowments: faith in a "double portion," along with "vision and discernment" to speak God's words concerning the kingdom.
- Praise is offered to Jesus for His ultimate victory: "Hallelujah! Peace and praise belong to you Lord Jesus," acknowledging that He "triumphed the world when you were slain with no stain or disdain."
- A sharp contrast is drawn between heavenly treasure and earthly pursuits: the enemies "sowed their seeds with man-made seeds, not treasure from heaven but the things that parish away."
- The consequence of this worldly focus is noted: they have "given over to worship what parishes away."
- The sovereignty of God is asserted forcefully: "If you bring destruction, who can stand against you."

- Mercy is sought to save the people from the "frivolity of foolishness" and the actions of wicked men who operate in darkness.
- The specific acts of the oppressors are listed again: placing God's people in "chains, bondage," confining them in "camps," and scattering stolen children into the streets.
- The final military request is for celestial aid: "Send your angels of protection against the wars of destruction, to save your people."
- The prayer concludes with an eternal declaration of worship: "Praise and glory be to God for your throne is forever."

The prayer "Deliver Me" encapsulates a comprehensive spiritual journey from abject despair to confident reliance on divine promises. It meticulously details the suffering inflicted by a hateful, corrupting force, employing vivid imagery of sickness, siege warfare, and profound personal betrayal. Central to the supplicant's argument for deliverance is the unwavering citation of scriptural guarantees, particularly the comprehensive protection offered in Psalms 91 and the historical precedent of God's faithfulness to His covenant people, as seen in the lament of Jeremiah. The text transitions from recounting past and present agony—including the echoes of Rachel's weeping—to embracing future restoration, symbolized by agricultural renewal and the return from exile. Ultimately, the prayer anchors itself in the identity of Jesus Christ as the indispensable "Bread of Life" (John 6: 35), seeking not just physical safety but profound spiritual sustenance, purification, and the power to stand against the transient, destructive works of darkness, concluding with an affirmation of God's eternal, unchallengeable throne.

Chapter 6

Whole Heart

I present my body as a living sacrifice, make me holy and acceptable unto you Lord Jesus; please don't turn your face from me. I come with an open invitation to allow you into my heart with great gladness. Hallelujah! In the book of Revelations 3:20 "you said that you stand at the door and knock," you said that if I open up, that you would come in and sup with me. I seek you with my whole heart. I honor and adore you. Hallelujah! I will make a joyful noise unto the Lord; I will rejoice of your goodness. In your love I abide. You alone are God and I marvel at all your profound; I exalt your name above all others. Accept me into my rightful place in your kingdom that I can praise your name. If there be anything in me that is not of you, I hereby denounce my flesh. I will worship you in spirit as you are, and in truth as that you are truth.

Strengthen me that I may not defile or sway from your word according to:

Mark 12:30
And you shall love the Lord your God with all your heart and with all your soul and with all your mind and with all your strength.'

Deuteronomy 10:12 ESV / 14

"And now, Israel, what does the Lord your God require of you, but to fear the Lord your God, to walk in all his ways, to love him, to serve the Lord your God with all your heart and with all your soul,

Colossians 3:23-24 ESV

Whatever you do, work heartily, as for the Lord and not for men, knowing that from the Lord you will receive the inheritance as your reward. You are serving the Lord Christ.

Psalm 119:1-176 ESV

Blessed are those whose way is blameless, who walk in the law of the Lord! Blessed are those who keep his testimonies, who seek him with their whole heart, who also do no wrong, but walk in his ways! You have commanded your precepts to be kept diligently. Oh, that my ways may be steadfast in keeping your statutes! ...

1 Chronicles 28:9 ESV

"And you, Solomon my son, know the God of your father and serve him with a whole heart and with a willing mind, for the Lord searches all hearts and understands every plan and thought. If you seek him, he will be found by you, but if you forsake him, he will cast you off forever.

The Imperative of Wholehearted Devotion to the Lord

This prayer synthesizes a profound declaration of faith centered entirely on the concept of wholehearted devotion to the Lord Jesus Christ. It begins as a personal petition and commitment, presenting the believer's body as a living sacrifice and extending an open invitation for divine presence, referencing the promise found in Revelation 3:20. The core purpose of the text is to establish an unwavering commitment to worship, obedience, and service that encompasses every facet of human existence—mind, soul, strength, and heart. This commitment is rigorously supported and defined by direct scriptural citations from Mark, Deuteronomy, Colossians, Psalm 119, and 1 Chronicles, all reinforcing the singular requirement: that the relationship with God must be absolute, undivided, and diligently maintained through all actions and thoughts.

30-day Breakthrough Prayer

The central message of the prayer revolves around several interconnected themes, each demanding total dedication and adherence to divine command.

The Commitment to Living Sacrifice and Open Invitation

This initial section establishes the foundational posture of the worshipper, characterized by self-offering and eager reception of the divine presence.

- The believer initiates the declaration by presenting their physical being as a "living sacrifice," a complete offering intended to be made "holy and acceptable unto you Lord Jesus."
- A plea is made for continued divine favor, specifically requesting that the Lord "don't turn your face from me."
- The heart is offered freely, characterized by "great gladness," signifying an unforced and joyful acceptance of God's presence.
- This invitation is explicitly linked to the promise recorded in the book of Revelation 3:20, where the Lord states He "stand[s] at the door and knock[s]."
- The condition for fellowship is clearly stated: the believer must open the door, whereupon the Lord promises to "come in and sup with me," establishing an intimate communion.
- The seeker affirms the depth of their pursuit, declaring, "I seek you with my whole heart," alongside expressions of deep reverence: "I honor and adore you."
- Joyful worship is promised, including making a "joyful noise unto the Lord" and rejoicing specifically in the Lord's goodness.
- The worshipper acknowledges the singular divinity of the subject of devotion: "You alone are God."
- Admiration extends to the profound nature of God, and the name of the Lord is exalted "above all others."
- A request for acceptance into the "rightful place in your kingdom" is made, with the express purpose of praising the Lord's name therein.

- A critical act of purification is declared: any element within the self that is "not of you" is hereby denounced, specifically referencing the renunciation of the "flesh."
- The ultimate form of worship is defined as being conducted "in spirit as you are, and in truth as that you are truth," demanding authenticity aligned with divine reality.

The prayer transitions from personal declaration to the foundational scriptural mandates that define the scope of this required love, emphasizing that it must be comprehensive, leaving no part of the self-untouched by devotion.

- The mandate cited from Mark 12:30 requires the Lord your God to be loved with an absolute totality: With "all your heart." With "all your soul." With "all your mind." With "all your strength."
- The passage from Deuteronomy 10:12 further delineates the requirements placed upon Israel, which serve as a template for the believer's required conduct: The primary requirement is to "fear the Lord your God." This fear must manifest in action by walking "in all his ways." It requires loving Him, which is inseparable from serving Him. This service must also be rendered completely, using "all your heart and with all your soul."

The Standard of Diligent Work and Steadfast Obedience (Colossians 3:23-24 & Psalm 119)

This theme addresses how wholehearted devotion translates into daily activity and adherence to divine law, linking effort and obedience directly to eternal reward.

- " The ultimate perspective is eternal, as the believer is "knowing that from the Lord you will receive the inheritance as your reward." This work is explicitly identified as "serving the Lord Christ."

- Blessedness is attributed to those whose "way is blameless." These blessed individuals "walk in the law of the Lord." They are characterized by keeping His testimonies and, crucially, by seeking Him "with their whole heart." The absence of wrongdoing ("who also do no wrong") is linked to walking in His ways. The text notes that God has commanded His precepts to be kept "diligently." The prayerful aspiration expressed is for one's ways to be "steadfast in keeping your statutes."

The Searchlight of God and the Consequence of Seeking (1 Chronicles 28:9)

The final scriptural reference provides a powerful rationale for the necessity of wholeheartedness, highlighting God's omniscience regarding internal states and the definitive consequences of seeking or forsaking Him.

- The instruction given to Solomon serves as a universal directive: one must "know the God of your father and serve him."
- This service must be executed with two specific internal qualities: "with a whole heart and with a willing mind."
- The reason for requiring this totality is God's absolute knowledge: "for the Lord searches all hearts and understands every plan and thought."
- The outcome of this internal search is presented as a clear binary choice: If one seeks Him, "he will be found by you." Conversely, "if you forsake him, he will cast you off forever."

The prayer culminates in an undeniable assertion that a relationship with the Lord demands absolute, comprehensive, and active devotion across all dimensions of life. The key takeaway is the requirement for totality: love must engage the heart, soul, mind, and strength without reservation, mirroring the comprehensive nature of the divine command. This wholeheartedness is not merely an emotional state, but a demonstrable commitment reflected in diligent work performed for the Lord, adherence to His statutes, and a conscious renunciation of anything contrary to His truth. Ultimately, the text serves as both a prayer for strength to maintain this path and a solemn recognition that the eternal outcome hinges upon whether one seeks God with an undivided heart or chooses to forsake Him.

30-day Breakthrough Prayer

Chapter 7

Ordain this Day

Lord Jesus, on this day in lightness, ordain me in thy salvation of ministry with enlightenment, power and vision. Ordain me that I should be able to see and ordain my mouth that I shall be able to speak thy word, of thy kingdom.

You said in your word:

John 1:1-5
In the beginning was the Word, and the Word was with God, and the Word was God. / He was with God in the beginning. / Through Him all things were made, and without Him nothing was made that has been made.

You said in the beginning: "let there be light," Genesis 1:3 and I know it is you who was there when the light came from the darkness which was called by your Word.

Awaken my mental spiritual consciousness with divine wisdom of ancient knowledge. Empower and anoint me with thy presence. Ordain me in the power to cast out demons, demonic spirits, energies and attackers, lurkers, those who wait in darkness to destroy the temples of God. In the name, by the blood of Jesus. Cancel every attack of the enemy against my family, children, grandchildren, my body, health, mind, soul, my finance, vision, businesses and future.

Remove every negative thought, energy, emotion and obstacle, internal and external that weighs against my purpose to advance and excel. Show me goodness and kindness in thy favor that I can learn of the truth and what life's projections for me are in love and in your kingdom. Flush me from the burdens of heaviness that soils my heart with sadness and disbelief. Make me new, do a new thing. Take not away my birth of children nor concepts and align my protection and spiritual discernment. Let there be rebirth in my life, restoring the youth into my bones. Provide a spiritual circumcision of my heart that I may dance and be joyous. Prepare a way before me, laying a foundation of irrevocable stone and landscape as Jehovah Jireh, my provider. My dominance to depend on man was fallible and built of lies and deception, so I have learned and repent of my ignorance.

Provide me and my children with shelter, for they waited to displace us. They tore at my children and my life seeking to cipher our lives by evil and unjust works. They have taken council in secret to destroy your children from the earth. Many times, have they done this evil bringing no peace, my soul cries out to you to come now and help us fight, send your angels to protect us. Remove every block, rock and stone they have laid down to block and crush us. Enemies that I do not know surrounded to watch and help bring destruction to us without purpose. Let my enemies be crushed by the boulders they have used to destroy us. For in your Word you say in Mathew 16:17-20

King James Bible
And I say also unto thee, that thou art Peter, and upon this rock I will build my church; and the gates of hell shall not prevail against it.

New King James Version
And I also say to you that you are Peter, and on this rock, I will build My church, and the gates of Hades shall not prevail against it.

Build here Jesus so that they don't destroy my house. Let their curses return to their roots gutting out all unrighteousness and destructive tactics to harm your people. Let there be bread in my house.

In Matthew 4:4

30-day Breakthrough Prayer

Man shall not live on bread alone, but on every word that comes from the mouth of God

Allow your word to be my source, my strength that doesn't fail, nor fade nor famine. They have stolen our food and mean to provide, they have taken what didn't belong to them and robbed our inheritance for evil deeds. Repay them with their own evil and restore our wealth. Wherever it is that the wind shall direct, let it be you God directing, and leading the wind. Let you move forward with us with each order of step, place us into a place that cannot be shaken or destroyed by our enemies. Strengthen me that I shall move In Rhythm, Harmony, Peace, Respect, Season and Love. Bring your Truth as I place my trust in irrevocable unfailing unshakable hands. In Jesus name.

Comprehensive Declaration for Spiritual Ordination, Restoration, and Divine Protection

This prayer serves as an intensive, multi-faceted prayer and declaration titled "Ordain this Day: Rebuild and Restore my Temple." Its primary purpose is to invoke divine intervention for spiritual empowerment, comprehensive cleansing from negative influences, restoration of personal and familial well-being, and establishing an unshakeable foundation based on scriptural promises. The supplicant seeks ordination into salvation and ministry, requesting divine wisdom, the power to engage in spiritual warfare against demonic forces, and the removal of internal and external obstacles hindering their purpose. Furthermore, the declaration emphasizes repentance for past reliance on fallible human structures and demands the reversal of injustices, restoration of stolen resources, and assurance of continuous, divinely directed provision and protection for the supplicant and their descendants.

The Call for Divine Ordination and Ministry

- The supplicant begins by petitioning the Lord Jesus for ordination on this specific day, characterized by lightness.
- This ordination is sought specifically for salvation and ministry, requiring the infusion of enlightenment, power, and clear vision.
- A core request is the ordination of the supplicant’s mouth, enabling them to see clearly and subsequently speak the divine word pertaining to God's kingdom.
- The desire is to be equipped to function effectively within a ministry context, empowered by divine presence and understanding.
- This initial appeal sets the stage for a comprehensive request for spiritual equipping and authority to operate in the divine realm.

Grounding in Scriptural Authority: The Primacy of the Word

- The declaration anchors its authority by referencing the spoken word of God, specifically citing John 1:1-5.
- The text emphasizes the eternal nature of the Word, stating that in the beginning, the Word existed, was with God, and was God Himself.
- It highlights the Word's role as the agent of creation, affirming that through Him all things visible and invisible were made.
- A crucial point is the affirmation that nothing that has been made exists outside of the creative power of this Word.
- The declaration further recalls the initial creative command: "let there be light."
- The supplicant acknowledges that the Word is the source of that initial light, which successfully emerged from the preceding darkness.
- This recognition solidifies the belief that the Word spoken by God is the ultimate power capable of dispelling obscurity and establishing reality.

Spiritual Warfare and Deliverance from Darkness

30-day Breakthrough Prayer

- A fervent request is made to awaken the supplicant's mental and spiritual consciousness, seeking the infusion of divine wisdom derived from ancient knowledge.
- The supplicant asks to be empowered and anointed directly by the divine presence.
- A specific ordination is sought: the power to actively cast out various forms of spiritual opposition.
- This opposition is cataloged extensively, including demons, demonic spirits, negative energies, attackers, and lurkers that wait in darkness.
- The stated purpose of these entities is to destroy the temples of God, which the supplicant identifies as their own being and domain.
- The authority for this warfare is invoked specifically "In the name, by the blood of Jesus."
- The declaration moves to cancel every single attack launched by the enemy against specific areas of life.
- These targeted areas include the supplicant's family, children, and grandchildren.
- Furthermore, protection is sought for the supplicant's physical body, health, mind, and soul.
- The cancellation extends to the material aspects of life, specifically finance, vision, businesses, and the future trajectory of life.

Internal Cleansing and Renewal of the Heart

- The prayer calls for the removal of all internal and external obstacles, negative thoughts, negative energy, and negative emotions that actively weigh against the purpose to advance and excel.
- The supplicant seeks to experience goodness and kindness flowing from divine favor.
- This favor is desired so that the truth of God's projections for their life, rooted in love and within the kingdom, can be learned and embraced.

- A cleansing action is requested: to flush out the burdens of heaviness that currently soil the heart, manifesting as sadness and disbelief.
- The plea is for radical transformation: "Make me new, do a new thing."
- The supplicant asks that the blessing of having children or concepts related to progeny not be taken away, seeking alignment in protection and spiritual discernment.
- A profound request for physical and spiritual rejuvenation is made to experience rebirth in life, resulting in the restoration of youth into the bones.
- The declaration seeks a spiritual circumcision of the heart, which is desired so that the supplicant may experience uninhibited joy and dance.

Establishing Divine Foundation and Repentance

- The supplicant asks for the divine provider, Jehovah Jireh, to prepare a way forward.
- This preparation involves laying a foundation described as irrevocable stone and establishing a secure landscape.
- A significant moment of self-reflection and repentance is recorded, acknowledging past errors in reliance.
- The supplicant confesses that their previous reliance on human dominance was inherently fallible, built upon lies and deception.
- As a result of this realization, the supplicant expresses having learned from this ignorance and formally repents for it.
- The prayer transitions to immediate physical needs, asking for shelter for both the supplicant and their children.
- This request is framed against the threat of displacement, noting that enemies have actively sought to remove them.
- The text details the severity of the attack, stating that enemies have torn at the children and the supplicant's life, seeking to decipher or

unravel their existence through evil and unjust works.

Confronting Hidden Enemies and Seeking Angelic Intervention

- The prayer reveals that enemies have convened in secret councils with the specific intent to destroy God’s children from the earth.
- The supplicant notes that these evil actions have been repeated many times, consistently bringing no peace to the soul.
- In response, the soul cries out for immediate divine intervention to fight alongside them.
- A specific request is made for God to send angels to provide protection during this conflict.
- The prayer demands the removal of every physical and spiritual obstruction—every block, rock, and stone—that enemies have deliberately laid down to crush and impede progress.
- The presence of unknown enemies surrounding them, watching, and intending destruction without purpose is acknowledged.
- A powerful declaration of reversal is made that the enemies themselves be crushed by the very boulders and implements they intended to use for destruction.

The Foundation of the Church and Invulnerability

- The declaration reinforces its spiritual authority by citing specific promises from scripture regarding the establishment of God’s structure.
- The text quotes Matthew 16:17-20 from the King James Bible, emphasizing the declaration to Peter: "upon this rock I will build my church; and the gates of hell shall not prevail against it."
- It also references the New King James Version of the same passage, confirming that on this rock, the Church will be built, and the gates of Hades will not overcome it.

- Based on this divine promise, the supplicant issues a direct command: "Build here Jesus so that they don't destroy my house."
- This signifies a request for divine fortification of their dwelling place, making it impervious to enemy action.
- The prayer demands that any curses directed toward the supplicant or their people must return to their origins.
- This reversal must be thorough, "gutting out all unrighteousness and destructive tactics" aimed at harming God's people.

Reversal of Injustice and Sustenance by the Word

- A fundamental need for sustenance is declared: "Let there be bread in my house."
- This physical need is immediately linked to spiritual sustenance by referencing Matthew 4:4.
- The scriptural principle cited is that humanity shall not live on bread alone, but on every word that proceeds from the mouth of God.
- The supplicant asks that God's word become their primary source and strength, a resource that is guaranteed not to fail, fade, or lead to famine.
- The text addresses material theft and economic sabotage committed by adversaries.
- It states that enemies have stolen food and the means necessary for provision.
- The declaration asserts that these enemies have taken what rightfully belonged to the supplicant and have robbed their inheritance through their evil deeds.
- A demand for equitable justice is made: that these enemies be repaid with their own evil actions.
- Concurrently, the supplicant demands the full restoration of their wealth and possessions.

Restoration of Wealth and Movement Under Divine Guidance

- The prayer seeks absolute divine direction for all future movement and endeavors.

30-day Breakthrough Prayer

- The supplicant requests that wherever the wind might direct them, it must, in fact, be God directing and leading that wind.
- There is a plea for God to move forward with the supplicant at every single order of step they take.
- This divine partnership is intended to place them in a location or state that cannot be shaken or destroyed by their enemies.
- The final requests focus on achieving internal and relational equilibrium through divine strengthening.
- The supplicant asks to be strengthened to move in a state characterized by Rhythm, Harmony, Peace, Respect, Season, and Love.
- The ultimate act of faith is declared: bringing God's Truth into reality as the supplicant places their complete trust in hands described as irrevocable, unfailing, and unshakable.
- The entire declaration is sealed with the invocation, "In Jesus name."

The document, "Ordain this Day: Rebuild and Restore my Temple," is a comprehensive spiritual petition characterized by intense focus on spiritual warfare, personal renewal, and material restoration. The key takeaways center on the absolute necessity of divine ordination for ministry, the foundational power of God's Word (as exemplified by John 1: 1-5 and Matthew 4:4), and the active cancellation of all spiritual attacks targeting the family, body, and finances. The supplicant demands radical internal transformation—shedding sadness and disbelief for spiritual circumcision and renewed youth—while simultaneously calling for the physical protection of their home and the reversal of curses and theft perpetrated by hidden enemies. By invoking the promise made to Peter (Matthew 16: 17-20), the prayer seeks to establish an unshakeable foundation, concluding with a commitment to move forward only under the direct, harmonious guidance of God, placing all trust in His unfailing power.

30-day Breakthrough Prayer

30-day Breakthrough Prayer

Chapter 8

Beauty of the Lilies

How long Lord will you look upon the prosperity of the wicked.

How long will you look and see the just forsaken.

It's time for you to act, it is time to bring refuge to your people against them that do wrong.

The rich people have created a hardship of oppression, and many suffer because of the greed of governance and misappropriation of the land resources. They claim ownership of the plentiful that you have given unto us. They withhold dew season and have no rational to feed the people. They use systems to decide who eats, which do not feed the children.

Many are sleep upon the streets, awaken me from slumber, stand me up firmly that I shall not be moved, shaken up, or cast away. Bring justice that those who do unrighteousness, Shalom. Slay them with judgement in your courts, them that do evil. Disrupt the deeds of evil they conjure in their secret; plans to slaughter your people.

I come from a blessed seed, and they shall call me blessed, I will forever be blessed.

Is it that this land you have given to the heathen, or that all things belong to you?

As I go through my journey Lord, let me not beg for bread, allow us to see the beauty of the Lilies of the field.

They have developed inequality and stripped us of our roots and heritage, let the enemy not eat of my inheritance. You are a God that provides, Jehovah Jireh, my provider. Hallelujah! Many have become lost and scorn, but you show me great mercies. Take favor unto me, that I tell how you delighted in me. Hallelujah!

30-day Breakthrough Prayer

I sought you when I was young, you know the hair count of my head, you knitted me together when I was still in my mothers womb. Many days was my sorrow when I had backslider, because my feet did slip; I followed the way of darkness, and it ripped away at my soul. The entanglements had surrounded me, but it was you who pulled me out of the trap they set to destroy me.

In darkness they waited, that they should place their cords around my children.

But you are a God that brings righteousness, and deliverance to your people.

May you recover my seed that nothing should harm, destroy, or overtake them.

Nothing will subdue me, bring your judgment and justice to refrain me from the enemies.

What is this place that prosecute and abhor the righteousness?

They give rewards to the murderers, those who harm children and lead them astray.

Remove the curtain for all to see the evil works they obtain, rescue me from evil men.

It is you who I look to for vengeance and you who provide magnitude. Bring Order and justice and bless your children. Refrain chaos and confusion far from me, Shalom, prince of peace is risen. Many have been my days of torment; the time is now that I arise to defend myself so that I may claim liberty.

Hear my prayers, bring it to past and I shall sing of your glory.

I will tell the people how the Lord Jesus established me. Hallelujah!

Amen.

A Lament and Plea for Divine Justice: An Examination of the Beauty of the Lilies

30-day Breakthrough Prayer

This document, titled "Beauty of the Lilies," presents a profound and impassioned lyrical prayer directed toward the Lord. It serves as a multifaceted expression of suffering, social critique, and unwavering faith. The text details severe grievances against the powerful elite who exploit resources and oppress the vulnerable, contrasting this worldly corruption with a deep personal reliance on divine mercy and intervention. The core purpose is to petition for immediate justice, protection for the faithful, and ultimate deliverance from the forces of evil and unrighteousness that plague the speaker and their community. The narrative moves from observation of systemic failure to personal testimony of past darkness and present reliance on divine power, culminating in a final declaration of faith and hope for peace.

The Cry Against Worldly Prosperity and Systemic Injustice

This section details, the speakers distress regarding the current situation, where the wicked thrive where the righteous suffer, driven by the greed and malfeasance of the wealthy and governing bodies.

- Questioning Divine Patience Regarding Wicked Prosperity: The prayer begins with an urgent, rhetorical questioning of the Lord, demanding to know how much longer divine attention will be focused upon the successful and prosperous nature of the wicked individuals who operate without consequence in the world.
- Lament for the Forsaken Just: Simultaneously, the speaker expresses deep sorrow over the prolonged state of abandonment felt by those who strive to live righteously, asking how long they must endure being overlooked and left without aid while injustice prevails.
- The Need for Immediate Divine Action: There is a clear declaration that the time for passive observation has ended, emphasizing the critical

necessity for the Lord to intervene swiftly and decisively to bring forth refuge and protection for the people against all those who actively commit wrongdoing.

- Condemnation of Rich People's Oppression: The text explicitly identifies the rich as the architects of widespread hardship, noting that their actions breed oppression that causes immense suffering across the community.
- Critique of Governance and Resource Misappropriation: This suffering is directly linked to the greed inherent in governance structures, specifically citing the misappropriation and selfish control over vital land resources that rightfully belong to the populace.
- Claiming Ownership of God-Given Abundance: The powerful are accused of arrogantly claiming ownership over the plentiful resources that the Lord has bestowed upon all people, thereby hoarding what should be shared.
- Withholding Essential Sustenance: A specific act of cruelty detailed is the withholding of the "dew season," symbolizing the intentional denial of necessary provisions, demonstrating a complete lack of rational concern for the feeding and survival of the general population.
- The Cruelty of Slavery Methods in Distribution: The speaker condemns the use of oppressive, slavery-like methods to determine who receives food, highlighting the tragic outcome that even children are left unfed by this unjust system.
- Personal Experience of Homelessness and Displacement: The depth of the crisis is made personal, as the speaker reveals that many are forced to sleep upon the streets, including the speaker themselves, who has suffered the ultimate indignity of being tossed out of their own home.
- The Stripping of Heritage and Roots: Further detailing the systemic damage, the text notes that these oppressive forces have actively developed inequality and systematically stripped the people

of their foundational heritage and ancestral roots, leading to cultural erosion.
- The State of Being Lost and Scorned: As a consequence of this oppression and cultural stripping, many individuals have become lost in despair and subjected to scorn, though the speaker acknowledges that the Lord has shown them great mercies despite this environment.

The Demand for Divine Retribution and Legal Judgment

This theme focuses on the speaker's fervent prayers for God to enact judgment, disrupt evil schemes, and establish righteousness through authoritative action.

- Call for Justice in the Courts of Heaven: The speaker demands that justice be brought forth against those who commit unrighteous acts, specifically requesting that they be "slain with judgement in your courts," signifying a desire for ultimate, authoritative condemnation.
- Disruption of Secret Evil Conspiracies: A direct plea is made for the Lord to intervene and disrupt the secret, hidden deeds and plans that evildoers conjure up with the malicious intent of slaughtering the Lord's people.
- Questioning the Land's Allegiance: The speaker poses a profound theological question regarding the ownership of the land, asking if it has been given over to the heathen, or if, in truth, all things ultimately belong to the Lord, implying that ownership should reflect divine will.
- A Plea for Sustenance Over Begging: As the journey through life continues, the speaker requests that they and their people be spared the humiliation of begging for bread, instead asking to witness the divine beauty found in the "Lilies of the field" as a sign of provision.
- A Declaration of Blessed Lineage: The speaker asserts their own spiritual standing, asking the Lord to recognize that they come from a "blessed seed," and in response, to declare them blessed in return.

- The Need for Judgment Against Persecutors: The prayer explicitly asks what kind of societal structure exists where righteousness is prosecuted and abhorred, highlighting the moral inversion of the current system.
- Condemnation of Rewarding Evil: The text concludes this section of grievance by pointing out the perverse reward system in place, where murderers and those who harm and lead children astray are instead given rewards by the earthly powers.
- Seeking Vengeance and Magnitude: The speaker explicitly looks to the Lord as the source for vengeance against their enemies and the provider of the necessary magnitude or power to enact this justice.
- A Call for Order, Justice, and Blessing: A direct command or strong petition is issued for the Lord to bring forth definitive Order and justice, and to bestow blessings upon the children of the faithful.
- Request for Repulsion of Chaos: The speaker asks that chaos and confusion be forcefully restrained and kept far away from them, invoking the title "Shalom, prince of peace" as the desired state of being.

Personal History of Spiritual Struggle and Redemption

This section shifts focus inward, detailing the speaker's personal journey through darkness, temptation, and the subsequent rescue provided by divine intervention.

- Sorrow During Youth and Spiritual Stumbling: The speaker recounts a time of deep sorrow experienced when they were young and felt locked away or constrained, admitting that their "feet did slip."
- Following the Path of Darkness: This stumbling led the speaker down a destructive path, acknowledging that they followed "the way of darkness," which resulted in severe spiritual damage that "ripped at my soul."

- Entanglements and Divine Rescue: Despite being surrounded by complex spiritual or worldly entanglements designed to trap them, the speaker testifies that it was the Lord who actively pulled them out of the trap set specifically to destroy them.
- Waiting in Darkness for the Next Attack: The speaker notes that the enemies waited in the darkness, poised to place their "cords around my children," indicating a continuous threat to the next generation.
- Affirmation of God as Deliverer: In contrast to the enemy's plans, the speaker affirms the true nature of their God: one who reliably brings forth righteousness and deliverance to His people.
- Prayer for the Recovery and Protection of Seed: A specific, heartfelt prayer is offered for the recovery of the speaker's "seed" (offspring or legacy), asking that nothing in the world be allowed to harm, destroy, or overtake them.
- Declaration of Unsubduable Faith: The speaker declares a state of spiritual resilience, asserting that "Nothing will subdue us," and requests that God's judgment and justice be brought forth to restrain them from the influence of the enemy.

The Pursuit of Spiritual Sustenance and Final Deliverance

The final segment focuses on requests for clarity, liberty, and the ultimate declaration of established faith in the Lord Jesus.

- Request for Revelation of Evil Works: The speaker asks for a divine unveiling, requesting that the curtain be removed so that all can clearly see the evil works that their adversaries have managed to obtain, demanding exposure for these hidden machinations.
- Plea for Rescue from Evil Men: Following the exposure of evil, the speaker asks directly to be rescued from the presence and influence of these evil men.

- The Long Wait for Liberty: The speaker reflects on the duration of their trials, noting that they have endured "many days of torrent," and expresses the deep yearning to finally place their feet into liberty, implying a current state of constraint.
- Hope for Fulfillment of Prayers: The text expresses hope that the Lord will heed their prayers and bring the desired outcomes to pass, promising that upon this fulfillment, the speaker will sing of God's glory.
- Aspiration to Witness and Proclaim Faith: The ultimate goal articulated is the desire to publicly testify and tell the people how the Lord Jesus Christ established the speaker in their faith and position.
- Request for Past Sorrows to End: The speaker asks that the difficulties and torrents experienced be brought to the past, signifying a desire for closure on the period of suffering.
- Seeking Clarity Through Divine Sight: There is a poignant request that the Lord place their eyes in a position where they can see liberty, suggesting that true freedom begins with a shift in spiritual perspective or divine favor.
- The Desire to See Evil Works Obvious: Reiterating the need for clarity, the speaker wants the evil works obtained by their adversaries to be made completely visible to everyone.
- The Need for Protection from Harm: A continuous thread is the need for recovery and protection for the speaker's descendants, ensuring that no external force can harm or overtake them.
- The Final Affirmation of Establishment: The prayer concludes with a powerful declaration of certainty, stating the intention to inform the public precisely how the Lord Jesus established the speaker's standing and faith.

The prayer "Beauty of the Lilies" functions as a comprehensive spiritual and social testament, weaving together sharp critiques of worldly corruption with profound personal appeals for divine intervention. The central takeaway is the urgent demand for justice against a system characterized by the rich hoarding resources, oppressing the poor, and rewarding wickedness, while the righteous suffer neglect and displacement. The speaker moves from lamenting systemic failure—including resource deprivation and cultural stripping—to recounting a personal history of falling into darkness and being miraculously rescued by the Lord's power. The prayer is saturated with requests for judgment, protection for future generations, and the establishment of divine order (Shalom). Ultimately, the text is a declaration of enduring faith, culminating in the hope that through God's intervention, the speaker will be granted liberty and the opportunity to publicly proclaim the glory and establishing power of the Lord Jesus Christ to the people. The entire work underscores the belief that true provision and peace are found not in earthly prosperity, but in divine righteousness.

30-day Breakthrough Prayer

Chapter 9

Soul Cry

Untie the knots, break the yokes and unmask the masked, exposing those that prosper in their evil ways, scheme, plot and connive wicked scams and manipulate the widows and children and cut the cords of evil attacks and dark lurkers of destruction completely into great distances far from east to west, far from below, far from me and my seed. Keep me above and they that seek and wait to mark injustices upon us, let them vanish into dust, my soul cries out to you lord. Oh, my soul, I cry loud, hear my cry, oh soul, I cry out loud to the Heavens. Hear my cry.

They made me their target to carry out their schemes, take back my life from their hearts and restore what they have stolen unto me. Your protection is being sought by me, rescue me from the many men that do not know you, nor wait for your voice. They do not answer to you, their father is of deceit, of lies, and the evil one.

Let them not vomit me out like the spirits they drink into their souls until they become sickened and aloof. Save me from the attack of evil men.

I look on every side, and they had placed dishonesty, betrayers and enemies that I did and did not know to swallow me up. They used system to tyrant and scale up their walls to lure me into trouble. They planted false friends and those who I knew to betray me. The were enticed with treasures to do the evil deeds that would destroy my soul. Even the children did they seek. They laughed when i mourned. They took the food off my table and cast me out of my home; they used my possessions as charity to spite me. My tears became their pleasure. Save me lord Jesus, oh, God my soul cries out to the heavens, let me not be scorn.

Blind the watchmen with distorted vision, interpretation and disconnection, bring malfunction and confusion to the systems concerning my business. No weapon formed against me shall prosper, cancel their assignment setting them beneath my rising up.

Vindicate my name, reputation, my purpose, my heart, my seed. Make a path straight before me. Show me thy favor and lead me assurity away from your reproach.

If it is your anger that I have provoked, have mercy and refrain from anger. I have turned my ways and look to the hill from where my help comes. I have not bowed my head to any false idols, yet I am scorned.

Bring me your daily bread, that my mental, emotional, physical needs are met. Let the pain dissipate. Pain is gone.

How long will you look upon my misery, I pray the mercy of your joy to fill my spirit and hearken to my cries, oh my soul cry's out? Restore my soul and bring youth into my bones. In the heartfelt of my soul, I cry unto the Lord. In Jesus name.

Amen.

A Comprehensive Exegesis of the Soul's Lament and Plea for Deliverance

This document, titled "Soul Cry," serves as an intense, deeply personal supplication directed toward a divine authority, expressing profound suffering, betrayal, and a desperate need for immediate intervention and vindication. The text chronicles the speaker's experience of being targeted by malicious forces—both known and unknown—who have engaged in systemic oppression, theft, emotional torment, and spiritual warfare. The core purpose of this prayer is to articulate the depth of this anguish, demand the dismantling of the enemies' schemes, seek physical and spiritual restoration, and ultimately secure divine favor and a clear path forward, away from reproach and scorn. It functions as a spiritual declaration against dark influences and a fervent request for justice and mercy.

The Demand for Unmasking and Dismantling of Evil Structures

This section details the speaker's initial, urgent demands for divine action to neutralize the sources of their affliction, focusing on exposure and the severing of spiritual and physical bonds of oppression.

- Untying Knots and Breaking Yokes: The speaker calls for the immediate dissolution of all binding constraints, symbolizing complex, interwoven problems or spiritual chains that restrict freedom and progress. This is a request for the fundamental undoing of established negative patterns imposed upon their life.
- Unmasking the Masked Perpetrators: A critical element of the plea is the requirement that those who prosper through deceitful means be publicly exposed. This demands that their hidden agendas and true natures be revealed, stripping them of any false pretense they maintain in society.
- Exposing Wicked Schemes and Conspiracies: The cry targets those who actively scheme, plot, and connive wicked scams. This suggests organized, premeditated malice rather than accidental misfortune, requiring targeted divine disruption of their planning stages.
- Protection for the Vulnerable: The speaker specifically highlights the enemies' manipulation of widows and children, underscoring the moral

depravity of the oppressors. The plea demands the cutting of the cords of evil attacks directed at these vulnerable parties, extending protection to the speaker's own lineage ("my seed").
- Complete Annihilation of Dark Forces: The request is for the total elimination of "dark lurkers of destruction," banishing them to "great distances," specifically defined across all cardinal directions (east to west, far from below), ensuring they are removed entirely from the speaker's sphere of influence.
- Ascension Above Adversaries: A desire is expressed to be kept elevated above those who actively wait and watch for opportunities to mark injustices upon the speaker, ensuring that these malicious observers are rendered powerless and vanish into dust.
- The Intensity of the Cry: The section culminates in the repeated, loud declaration of the soul's cry to the Lord and the Heavens, emphasizing the urgency and overwhelming nature of the distress that necessitates such a powerful appeal.

Targeting, Theft, and the Pursuit of Rescue

This theme focuses on the personal nature of the attack, the specific actions taken by the enemies, and the speaker's urgent need for physical and spiritual reclamation.

- Designation as a Primary Target: The speaker identifies themselves as the deliberate focus of the enemies' schemes, indicating a targeted campaign designed to undermine their existence and well-being.
- Restoration of Life and Stolen Assets: A central demand is the taking back of the speaker's life from the hearts of the oppressors, coupled with the explicit restoration of everything that has been stolen, implying significant material or spiritual loss.
- Seeking Protection from the Unconverted: The speaker explicitly seeks protection from "many men

that do not know you," highlighting a spiritual divide. These individuals are characterized by their refusal to heed divine voice or authority.

- Identification of the Enemy's Origin: The enemies are defined by their allegiance to deceit and lies, identified as being of "the evil one." This frames the conflict not just as a personal dispute but as a spiritual battle against forces opposed to truth.
- Deliverance from Spiritual Consumption: A visceral plea is made to avoid being "vomited out" like the spirits the enemies consume, suggesting the oppressors are engaging in dark spiritual practices that threaten to contaminate or expel the speaker if they are not saved.
- Urgent Salvation from Evil Men: The immediate need for rescue from the active "attack of evil men" is stressed, emphasizing that the danger is present and ongoing.

The Pain of Betrayal and Systemic Oppression

This extensive section details the specific methods of betrayal employed by enemies, encompassing both personal relationships and the manipulation of societal structures.

- Ubiquitous Hostility: The speaker describes looking in every direction only to find dishonesty, betrayers, and enemies, suggesting a pervasive atmosphere of threat from both known and unknown sources intended to "swallow me up."
- Manipulation of Systems for Tyranny: The enemies utilized established systems to exert tyrannical control and erected metaphorical walls ("scale up their walls") specifically designed to lure the speaker into inescapable trouble.
- The Treachery of False Friends: The pain is compounded by the actions of those perceived as friends, who were planted specifically to betray the speaker. These individuals were motivated by external rewards.

- Enticement by Material Treasures: The betrayers were lured into committing destructive acts against the speaker's soul by the promise of treasures, illustrating a trade of loyalty for material gain.
- Cruelty Extending to Family: The depth of the malice is shown by the fact that the enemies even sought to harm the speaker's children, indicating a complete lack of moral restraint.
- Derision in Times of Grief: The oppressors derived pleasure from the speaker's suffering, specifically laughing when the speaker mourned, highlighting emotional sadism.
- Deprivation and Humiliation: Concrete acts of cruelty are listed: having food taken from the table, being cast out of their own home, and having personal possessions cynically repurposed as "charity" intended solely to spite the speaker.
- Tears as Entertainment: The speaker notes that their tears became the pleasure and satisfaction of their tormentors, emphasizing the psychological torture inflicted.
- A Specific Appeal to Jesus: The distress leads to a direct invocation of "lord Jesus," reinforcing the spiritual nature of the plea and the desire not to be subjected to further scorn.

Warfare Against Oversight and Business Malfunction

This theme shifts focus to disrupting the mechanisms of control and surveillance used by the opposition, particularly concerning professional or business endeavors.

- Blinding the Watchmen: The speaker prays for divine interference against those acting as overseers or authorities ("watchmen"). This interference must manifest as distorted vision, flawed interpretation, and complete disconnection from reality.
- Inflicting Confusion on Systems: A specific request is made to bring malfunction and confusion into the systems that govern the speaker's

business affairs, thereby neutralizing their operational effectiveness.

- Affirmation of Divine Protection: The speaker invokes the spiritual law that "No weapon formed against me shall prosper," asserting an inherent shield against all offensive efforts directed their way.
- Cancellation of Assignments: The prayer demands the cancellation of the enemies assigned tasks or spiritual mandates, ensuring that these negative directives are rendered inert beneath the speaker's inevitable success ("my rising up").

The Quest for Vindication and Favorable Guidance

This section outlines the desired outcome regarding the speaker's public standing and future direction, seeking restoration of honor and clear divine favor.

- Vindication of Identity: The speaker seeks public vindication for every facet of their being: their name, their reputation, their divine purpose, the integrity of their heart, and the future of their seed.
- Establishment of a Straight Path: A request is made for divine assistance in making the path forward clear and unobstructed, removing the obstacles and deceptions planted by enemies.
- Manifestation of Favor: The speaker asks to be shown divine favor, which serves as a tangible sign of acceptance and protection.
- Assured Movement Away from Reproach: The final request in this area is for guidance that leads with "assurity" away from any remaining sense of reproach or public shame.

Seeking Mercy and Acknowledging Spiritual Stance

Turning inward and upward, the speaker addresses the potential role of their own actions in provoking divine displeasure, while simultaneously asserting their faithfulness.

- Plea for Mercy Over Anger: The speaker acknowledges the possibility that their actions may have provoked divine anger and immediately pleads for mercy, asking that this anger be refrained.
- Repentance and Redirection: In response to perceived transgression, the speaker declares a turning away from past ways and a conscious redirection of focus toward the source of help ("the hill").
- Assertion of Idolatry Avoidance: Despite the suffering and scorn experienced, the speaker affirms a critical point of integrity: they have "not bowed my head to any false idols," suggesting that the suffering is undeserved based on their adherence to true worship.
- The Paradox of Scorn: The text highlights the painful contradiction: having maintained faithfulness, yet still enduring scorn from the world.

Provision, Healing, and Dissipation of Pain

This theme focuses on immediate, tangible needs for sustenance and the cessation of ongoing suffering, encompassing physical, mental, and emotional well-being.

- Request for Daily Sustenance: The speaker asks for the provision of "daily bread," interpreted broadly to ensure that all essential needs—mental clarity, emotional stability, and physical requirements—are adequately met.
- Mandate for Pain Cessation: There is a direct command or fervent wish for the current pain to dissipate completely, followed by the declarative statement, "Pain is gone," indicating a strong expectation of immediate relief.

The Final Cry for Endurance and Restoration

The closing thoughts express a sense of weariness under prolonged suffering and conclude with a profound prayer for complete spiritual and physical renewal.

- Questioning the Duration of Misery: The speaker voices exhaustion by asking, "How long will you look upon my misery," indicating that the period of suffering has been extensive and taxing.
- Prayer for Joyful Filling: The speaker prays specifically for the mercy of joy to permeate their spirit, counteracting the misery they have endured.
- Heeding the Soul's Outcry: There is a plea for the divine ear to "hearken to my cries," acknowledging that the soul itself is actively crying out for attention.
- Ultimate Restoration: The prayer concludes with the ultimate requests: to restore the soul entirely and to infuse the physical body with renewed vitality, symbolized by bringing "youth into my bones."

The "Soul Cry" prayer is a comprehensive spiritual inventory of affliction, betrayal, and warfare. It moves systematically from demanding the exposure and destruction of external evil structures to pleading for personal rescue from targeted attacks orchestrated by deceitful individuals motivated by material gain and malice. The speaker details profound personal losses—home, possessions, reputation—and the emotional devastation caused by false friends and systemic manipulation. Crucially, the cry balances intense demands for justice (blinding watchmen, canceling assignments) with humble acknowledgments of potential fault and assertions of spiritual fidelity (avoiding idols). The overarching takeaway is an urgent, multifaceted prayer for total restoration: the vindication of identity, the cessation of physical and emotional pain, the assurance of provision, and the infusion of renewed spiritual and physical vigor, all sought through divine favor and intervention against overwhelming opposition.

30-day Breakthrough Prayer

Chapter 10

Be Blessed

My sovereign Lord, I give my soul to you. I thank you for your tender mercy, loving me beyond my shortcomings. Blot out my transgressions. You have gifted me with the greatness of quest and conquer. Many tares did I fault; yet you didn't count them all, only that I gather experience that gains me lessons of advancement into deeper understanding. Bring forth the strength that produces change in every needed area to align my growth. In all things, you exist, in all things you obtain, may your wisdom correct me to truth and obedience to sustain away from trouble. Today, rebuild and restore my youth that I may bring you glory and that my children will also believe in your goodness, grace and the power of your mighty arm, show me your love and kindness.

Forgive me for my ignorance and wasteful judgment that I do not forsake being blessed and capable of multiplying what you provide. Rest my heart to make peace with what has passed away, quicken my mind, body, and soul with love, light and life to live in abundance never to lack or lose sight of the gift of joy. Take away every taste of poison from my heart, mind, body, soul, and habits.

Deuteronomy 28:1-7

And it shall come to pass, if thou shalt hearken diligently unto the voice of the Lord thy God, to observe and to do all his commandments which I command thee this day, that the Lord thy God will set thee on high above all nations of the earth:

2 And all these blessings shall come on thee, and overtake thee, if thou shalt hearken unto the voice of the Lord thy God.

3 Blessed shalt thou be in the city, and blessed shalt thou be in the field.

4 Blessed shall be the fruit of thy body, and the fruit of thy ground, and the fruit of thy cattle,

the increase of thy kine, and the flocks of thy sheep.

5 Blessed shall be thy basket and thy store.

6 Blessed shalt thou be when thou comest in, and blessed shalt thou be when thou goest out.

7 The Lord shall cause thine enemies that rise up against thee to be smitten before thy face: they shall come out against thee one way and flee before thee seven ways.

8 The Lord shall command the blessing upon thee in thy storehouses, and in all that thou settest thine hand unto; and he shall bless thee in the land which the Lord thy God giveth thee.

9 The Lord shall establish thee a holy people unto himself, as he hath sworn unto thee, if thou shalt keep the commandments of the Lord thy God, and walk in his ways.

Amen.

A Comprehensive Examination of Blessing, Obedience, and Divine Restoration

This document, titled "Be Blessed," presents a dual focus: first, a deeply personal and devotional prayer seeking forgiveness, restoration, and alignment with divine wisdom; and second, a foundational scriptural excerpt from Deuteronomy Chapter 28, which outlines the conditional promises of abundant blessings contingent upon diligent obedience to the voice and commandments of the Lord God. The document serves as both a petition for personal renewal and a reminder of the covenantal relationship between the divine and the faithful, emphasizing that comprehensive prosperity, protection, and establishment as a holy people are directly linked to adherence to divine law. The text moves from introspection and the request for purification to the external, tangible rewards promised for faithfulness, covering blessings in every aspect of life, from personal well-being and material wealth to victory over opposition and ultimate covenant fulfillment.

Personal Supplication for Mercy, Growth, and Restoration

The initial section of the document is a profound expression of faith directed toward a "sovereign Lord," characterized by deep gratitude and a request for cleansing and renewal. This theme explores the petitioner's acknowledgment of divine mercy, the recognition of personal failings, and the earnest desire for spiritual and physical revitalization.

- Acknowledgment of Tender Mercy and Transgression: The prayer begins by offering the soul to the Lord, expressing profound thanks for a "tender mercy" that extends beyond the recognition of the individual's inherent shortcomings. This mercy is acknowledged as a foundational grace, prompting an immediate request for the blotting out of transgressions, signifying a desire for complete spiritual absolution and a fresh start unburdened by past errors.
- Divine Gifting and the Experience of Learning: The petitioner recognizes that they have been gifted with the "greatness of quest and conquer." However, this journey is acknowledged to be imperfect, marked by the presence of "many tares" or faults. Crucially, the Lord is credited with not counting every fault, allowing the individual to gather essential experience. This experience is framed not as failure, but as the necessary mechanism for advancement, leading to deeper understanding and fostering the internal strength

required to enact change in every necessary area of life to align with divine growth patterns.

- The Pursuit of Wisdom and Obedience: A central plea involves the request for divine wisdom to act as a corrective force. This wisdom is sought to guide the individual toward truth and foster an unwavering obedience, which serves as the primary defense mechanism to sustain them away from trouble and adversity. The reliance on divine insight over personal judgment is paramount for navigating life's challenges successfully.
- Petition for Renewal and Legacy: The prayer transitions into a specific request for physical and spiritual rejuvenation: to "rebuild and restore my youth." This restoration is sought not for selfish gain, but explicitly so that the petitioner may bring glory to the Lord. Furthermore, this desire extends generationally, hoping that the petitioner's children will also come to believe in the "goodness, grace and power of your mighty hands," thereby ensuring the continuation of faith and the demonstration of divine love and kindness across the family line.
- Forgiveness for Ignorance and the Desire for Multiplicative Blessing: The petitioner seeks forgiveness for past "ignorance and wasteful judgment," specifically acknowledging the failure to fully embrace the capacity to be blessed and, critically, the ability to multiply what the Lord provides. This suggests an understanding that blessing is not merely passive reception but requires active stewardship and multiplication.
- Internal Purification and Abundance: A core request focuses on achieving internal peace regarding past events ("make peace with what has passed way"). This is coupled with an urgent plea for quickening the mind, body, and soul with "love, light and life." The ultimate goal of this revitalization is to live in a state of abundance, ensuring they never lack nor lose sight of the "gift of joy." The prayer culminates in a powerful request for the removal of all negative

influences, asking the Lord to "Take away every taste of poison from my heart, mind, body, soul and habits," signifying a comprehensive desire for holistic purification.

The Covenant of Diligent Obedience and National Elevation (Deuteronomy 28:1-2)

This section shifts focus to the explicit terms laid out in Deuteronomy, establishing the foundational principle that blessings are conditional upon diligent adherence to divine instruction.

- The Prerequisite of Diligent Hearkening: The text establishes a clear condition: "if thou shalt hearken diligently unto the voice of the Lord thy God." This emphasizes that mere hearing is insufficient; active, focused, and persistent attention to the divine voice is mandatory. This diligence must be coupled with the commitment "to observe and to do all his commandments" as commanded on that specific day.
- The Promise of Supreme Elevation: The direct consequence of fulfilling this prerequisite is a monumental promise: "that the Lord thy God will set thee on high above all nations of the earth." This speaks to a position of unparalleled honor, influence, and distinction granted by divine decree, setting the obedient people apart globally.
- The Overtaking Nature of Blessings: Verse 2 reinforces the certainty of the reward, stating that "all these blessings shall come on thee, and overtake thee." The use of the word "overtake" suggests a pervasive, inescapable flow of divine favor that pursues and envelops the faithful, provided they continue to hearken to the Lord’s voice.

Comprehensive Blessings in Daily Life and Environment (Deuteronomy 28:3-6)

These verses detail the specific, tangible domains where the promised blessings will manifest, covering location, productivity, material stores, and movement.

- Blessings in Place and Field: The blessings are not confined to one sphere but are universal in their application. The faithful shall be "Blessed shalt thou be in the city," indicating success and favor within organized communal life and commerce, and equally "blessed shalt thou be in the field," signifying prosperity in agricultural endeavors and connection to the land.
- Prosperity in Progeny and Produce: The divine favor extends directly to the continuation of life and the yield of the earth. Blessings are promised upon "the fruit of thy body" (children and descendants), "the fruit of thy ground" (crops), and "the fruit of thy cattle." This includes the increase of livestock, specifically mentioned as "the increase of thy Kine, and the flocks of thy sheep," ensuring generational wealth and sustenance through natural increase.
- Material Stores and Provisions: The blessing covers accumulated wealth and reserves. It is explicitly stated that "Blessed shall be thy basket and thy store," guaranteeing that both the containers used for daily needs (basket) and the long-term storage facilities (store) will be filled and protected.
- Blessings in Transition and Activity: The favor is constant, accompanying all movements and endeavors. The individual is blessed both when they arrive ("when thou comest in") and when they depart ("when thou goest out"). This suggests divine protection and success accompany all transitions, journeys, and daily activities, ensuring that no action is undertaken without the Lord's favor attached to it.

Divine Protection and Victory Over Adversaries (Deuteronomy 28:7)

30-day Breakthrough Prayer

This crucial verse addresses the aspect of security and military or competitive success, promising that the Lord Himself will actively intervene on behalf of the obedient.

- Active Smiting of Enemies: The Lord promises to actively cause enemies who rise up against the faithful to be "smitten before thy face." This implies a direct, visible, and undeniable demonstration of divine power protecting the individual, ensuring that confrontations result in immediate defeat for the opposition.
- The Magnitude of Flight: The nature of this victory is quantified for emphasis: enemies shall advance against the faithful in "one way" (a unified front) but shall flee in disarray "before thee seven ways." This hyperbolic expression signifies total rout, confusion, and widespread dispersal among the adversaries, demonstrating overwhelming divine superiority in conflict.

Blessings on Labor, Storage, and Inheritance (Deuteronomy 28:8)

Chapter 11

Seeking God's Kingdom

Seek ye first the kingdom of God, and His righteousness and all things will be added unto you, "Matthew 6:33". I seek you Lord now, do not hide yourself from me. Do not turn your face from me. I seek you in spirit and in truth. Precious Lamb, the risen savior who sits above the throne of all other kingdoms, Christ Jesus, It is you that I seek, the presence of my God whom descended into hell, having taken the keys of death, ascended into the kingdom of heaven and left with us the divine spirit of the Holy Ghost whom I refer to as comforter. Allow the Holy Spirit to gush into me with power and anointing; my spirit is to receive. Perform your spiritual circumcision on my life to bring spiritual alignment and purification within this temple; if it be anything unlike you that dwell inside me, let it be nullified, let it be cast down so that I am renewed and confirmed by the power of your might and spiritual atonement. Build up into me kingdom principles and mentality so that I establish my rightful place to exercise authority and dominion upon the earth as was your original ordination upon creation for me to acquire. Because you have all power, allow no other powers or principalities to dominate my purpose, but with your mighty arm, pull down each stronghold.

Increase my wisdom in double portions, provide me with unwavering faith for in your word which you are, and was from the beginning. In the beginning was the word, and the word was with you. You spoke all things into its existence. Hebrews 6:13 "but without Faith it is impossible to please him. For he that come to God, must believe that he is, and that He is a rewarder for those who diligently seek him."

This petition is upon my hearts request; in your word I utter Isaiah 55:6 "Seek the LORD while he may be found; call on him while he is near." I call out to the Heavens above all realms of all other kingdoms that you allow to abide, I come before your throne bowed down to receive your answer, authority and power to execute this calling upon my life.

Psalms 27:4

4 One thing have I desired of the Lord, that will I seek after; that I may dwell in the house of the Lord all the days of my life, to behold the beauty of the Lord, and to enquire in his temple.

The Profound Petition for Seeking God's Kingdom

This prayer presents a deeply personal and comprehensive spiritual petition, structured as an earnest prayer rooted in several key scriptural foundations, including Matthew 6:33, Hebrews 6:13, Isaiah 55:6, and Psalms 27:4. The core purpose of this text is to seek an immediate and unhindered relationship with the Lord, requesting divine empowerment through the Holy Spirit to facilitate spiritual alignment, purification, and the establishment of rightful authority on Earth. The petition moves sequentially from seeking the Kingdom and righteousness to requesting specific spiritual endowments—wisdom and unwavering faith—culminating in a declaration of the ultimate life goal: perpetual dwelling in the presence of God. It serves as a declaration of dependence upon divine power to overcome spiritual opposition and execute a specific calling upon the petitioner's life.

The Primacy of Seeking God's Kingdom and Righteousness

The foundation of this entire spiritual endeavor rests upon the explicit command and promise articulated in

30-day Breakthrough Prayer

Matthew 6:33: "Seek ye first the kingdom of God, and His righteousness and all things will be added unto you." This theme establishes the priority of the petition, demanding an immediate and focused pursuit of the Divine realm above all temporal concerns.

- The petitioner explicitly commands the Lord not to hide His face, signifying a desperate need for visible, tangible divine presence and acknowledgment.
- The seeking is defined as being conducted "in spirit and in truth," indicating a commitment to authenticity and a non-superficial engagement with the Divine.
- This seeking is directed specifically toward the "Precious Lamb, the risen savior who sits above the throne of all other kingdoms, Christ Jesus." This highlights the recognition of Christ's supreme sovereignty, positioning Him as the singular object of desire, even above the spiritual realms He conquered.
- The text recalls the pivotal acts of Christ: descending into hell, taking the keys of death, and ascending into the kingdom of heaven. This historical theological acknowledgment serves as the basis for the subsequent requests for power and authority, as the petitioner seeks alignment with the victor.
- The promise inherent in Matthew 6:33—that all other necessary things will be added—is implicitly trusted, meaning the pursuit of righteousness is not merely spiritual fulfillment but also the prerequisite for earthly provision and stability.
- The act of seeking is therefore understood as an active, ongoing process, requiring the petitioner to turn away from distractions and maintain an unwavering focus on the establishment of God's rule within their sphere of influence. This initial step frames all subsequent requests as secondary to, yet dependent upon, this primary alignment.

Direct Communion with the Risen Savior and Lord

30-day Breakthrough Prayer

A significant portion of the petition is dedicated to establishing a direct, unmediated connection with the person of Jesus Christ, recognizing Him as the source of all spiritual enablement.

- The petitioner identifies Christ Jesus as the ultimate object of the search, emphasizing the desire for His presence above all else.
- The text acknowledges the transfer of spiritual power following Christ's ascension, specifically referencing the "divine spirit of the Holy Ghost whom I refer to as comforter." This establishes the Holy Spirit as the immediate conduit through which the presence of the risen Savior is experienced in the present day.
- The request is for this Comforter to "gush into me with power and anointing," suggesting a desire for an overwhelming, unrestrained influx of divine energy, far beyond a mere trickle or subtle influence.
- The spirit of the petitioner is declared ready to receive this infusion, framing the self as a vessel prepared for divine occupation.
- The focus on the "risen savior" underscores the belief that the power being sought is resurrection power, capable of overcoming all forms of spiritual death, stagnation, or limitation within the believer's life.
- This communion is sought not just for personal comfort, but as the necessary precursor to fulfilling the mandate of authority and dominion mentioned later in the prayer.

The Impartation of the Holy Spirit and Spiritual Transformation

The prayer moves into specific demands for internal restructuring, utilizing powerful metaphors of spiritual surgery and renewal, all facilitated by the Holy Spirit.

- The central request here is for the Holy Spirit to "Perform your spiritual circumcision on my life." This concept implies a radical,

internal cutting away of that which is contrary to God's will, mirroring the Old Testament covenant sign but applied spiritually to the inner being.
- The goal of this circumcision is explicitly stated as bringing about "spiritual alignment and purification within this temple." The body and spirit are viewed as a sacred temple requiring constant maintenance and cleansing.
- There is a severe decree against any impurity: "if it be anything unlike you that dwell inside me, let it be nullified, let it be cast down." This demonstrates a zero-tolerance policy for spiritual contamination or influence that does not originate from the Divine.
- The desired outcome of this purification process is renewal and confirmation, achieved specifically "by the power of your might and spiritual atonement." This links the internal cleansing directly to the finished work of Christ on the cross.
  - This transformation is not passive; it is the necessary groundwork for the next stage of the petition—the building of kingdom structures within the self.

Establishing Earthly Dominion Through Kingdom Mentality

Having established the need for internal purity and divine anointing, the petitioner articulates the desire to translate this spiritual reality into tangible authority on Earth, fulfilling what is perceived as an original mandate.

- The prayer calls for the building up of "kingdom principles and mentality." This suggests a desire to adopt the operational framework, values, and mindset of God's eternal kingdom, replacing worldly or fleshly paradigms.
- The aim is to "establish my rightful place to exercise authority and dominion upon the earth." This authority is explicitly

linked back to the "original ordination upon creation for me to acquire," suggesting a desire to reclaim a lost or dormant inheritance granted at the dawn of time.

- A crucial element of this section is the recognition of spiritual warfare: "Because you have all power, allow no other powers or principalities to dominate my purpose." This acknowledges the reality of opposing spiritual forces seeking to usurp the petitioner's divinely appointed role.
- The reliance is placed entirely on divine strength to counter these forces: "but with your mighty arm, pull down each stronghold." The petitioner recognizes their own inability to dismantle these structures alone, requiring the overwhelming, irresistible force of God's power to achieve victory over entrenched opposition.
- This theme emphasizes that spiritual seeking is intrinsically linked to practical, authoritative living, where the internal alignment manifests externally as effective dominion.

The Pursuit of Enhanced Wisdom and Unwavering Faith

The petition shifts focus to specific intellectual and volitional endowments necessary for navigating the spiritual and earthly realms effectively—wisdom and faith.

- The request is specific: "Increase my wisdom in double portions." This echoes Old Testament concepts of receiving a magnified measure of divine insight, suggesting that current wisdom levels are insufficient for the tasks ahead.
- This wisdom must be coupled with "unwavering faith for in your word which you are." The faith requested is not merely belief, but a steadfast reliance on the eternal nature of God's spoken word, recognizing that the word

itself is God ("In the beginning was the word, and the word was with you").

- The text reinforces the necessity of this faith by quoting Hebrews 6:13: "but without Faith it is impossible to please him." This serves as a justification for the intensity of the request—the ability to please God is contingent upon this specific spiritual gift.
- Furthermore, the petitioner affirms the core tenets of faith required for approaching God: one must believe that God exists ("that he is") and that He actively rewards those who pursue Him diligently ("that He is a rewarder for those who diligently seek him").
- The concept of diligence is paramount here; the faith requested is not passive acceptance but an active, persistent seeking that merits divine recompense. This section solidifies the intellectual and volitional commitment required alongside the emotional and spiritual yearning expressed earlier.

Active Engagement in Seeking God According to Prophetic Call

This section details the active steps the petitioner is taking to engage the heavens, based on a specific prophetic utterance regarding accessibility to God.

- The current petition is framed as a direct response to a heartfelt request, which is then articulated through the word of Isaiah 55:6: "Seek the LORD while he may be found; call on him while he is near." This provides a temporal urgency to the entire exercise.
- The petitioner actively engages the spiritual geography: "I call out to the Heavens above all realms of all other kingdoms that you allow to abide." This implies a recognition that multiple spiritual jurisdictions exist, but the call is directed specifically to the highest authority that permits lesser realms to exist.

- The posture adopted before this authority is one of humility and submission: "I come before your throne bowed down." This contrasts sharply with the later request for authority, showing that the reception of power must follow an act of profound reverence.
- The purpose of this humble approach is explicitly transactional in a spiritual sense: "to receive your answer, authority and power to execute this calling upon my life." The petitioner is not merely asking for blessings, but for the tools—the mandate, the strength, and the authorization—to fulfill their designated purpose.
- This theme emphasizes that seeking is an active, vocal, and geographically aware spiritual engagement that demands a tangible response from the Divine Throne.

The final scriptural anchor, Psalms 27:4, defines the ultimate, non-negotiable aspiration that underpins all the preceding requests for power, wisdom, and authority.

- The petitioner declares this desire as the "One thing have I desired of the Lord, that will I seek after." This elevates the desire for communion above all other requests for provision or power.
- The specific nature of this dwelling is defined: "that I may dwell in the house of the Lord all the days of my life." This is not a temporary visit but a permanent state of residency within God's sanctuary.
- The purpose of this lifelong dwelling is experiential: "to behold the beauty of the Lord." This speaks to an unending appreciation and contemplation of God's inherent glory and perfection.
- Furthermore, this dwelling is active and intellectual: "and to enquire in his temple." This suggests that even in perpetual presence, the relationship remains dynamic, involving

ongoing learning, consultation, and revelation within the sacred space.

- All the preceding requests—for spiritual circumcision, dominion, wisdom, and power—are ultimately validated and contextualized by this final, overarching goal: ensuring that the life lived on Earth is one that leads directly and securely into eternal, intimate communion with the Divine.

Amen.

The prayer serves as a comprehensive blueprint for a life wholly dedicated to seeking and manifesting the Kingdom of God. It meticulously outlines a process beginning with the absolute prioritization of God's righteousness, followed by a fervent request for direct empowerment via the Holy Spirit, leading to internal purification and spiritual alignment. The prayer then transitions to the practical application of this power, demanding the dismantling of spiritual strongholds and the establishment of ordained earthly dominion based on a kingdom mentality. Crucially, this pursuit of authority is balanced by the need for enhanced wisdom and an unwavering, active faith, acknowledging that pleasing God is impossible without it. Every request for power, authority, and spiritual endowment is ultimately tethered to the singular, overarching desire expressed in Psalms 27: 4: a lifelong, intimate dwelling within the presence of the Lord to perpetually behold His beauty and seek His counsel. The entire petition is an integrated cycle of seeking, receiving, acting, and desiring deeper communion, all grounded in the victory of the Risen Savior.

30-day Breakthrough Prayer

The Profound Petition for Divine Presence, Authority, and Enduring Faith

This prayer presents a deeply personal and comprehensive spiritual petition, structured as an earnest prayer rooted in several key scriptural foundations, including Matthew 6:33, Hebrews 6:13, Isaiah 55:6, and Psalms 27:4. The core purpose of this text is to seek an immediate and unhindered relationship with the Lord, requesting divine empowerment through the Holy Spirit to facilitate spiritual alignment, purification, and the establishment of rightful authority on Earth. The petition moves sequentially from seeking the Kingdom and righteousness to requesting specific spiritual endowments—wisdom and unwavering faith—culminating in a declaration of the ultimate life goal: perpetual dwelling in the presence of God. It serves as a declaration of dependence upon divine power to overcome spiritual opposition and execute a specific calling upon the petitioner's life.

The Primacy of Seeking God's Kingdom and Righteousness

The foundation of this entire spiritual endeavor rests upon the explicit command and promise articulated in Matthew 6:33: "Seek ye first the kingdom of God, and His righteousness and all things will be added unto you." This theme establishes the priority of the petition, demanding an immediate and focused pursuit of the Divine realm above all temporal concerns.

- The petitioner explicitly commands the Lord not to hide His face, signifying a desperate need for visible, tangible divine presence and acknowledgment.
- The seeking is defined as being conducted "in spirit and in truth," indicating a commitment to authenticity and a non-superficial engagement with the Divine.

- This seeking is directed specifically toward the "Precious Lamb, the risen savior who sits above the throne of all other kingdoms, Christ Jesus." This highlights the recognition of Christ's supreme sovereignty, positioning Him as the singular object of desire, even above the spiritual realms He conquered.
- The text recalls the pivotal acts of Christ: descending into hell, taking the keys of death, and ascending into the kingdom of heaven. This historical theological acknowledgment serves as the basis for the subsequent requests for power and authority, as the petitioner seeks alignment with the victor.
- The promise inherent in Matthew 6:33—that all other necessary things will be added—is implicitly trusted, meaning the pursuit of righteousness is not merely spiritual fulfillment but also the prerequisite for earthly provision and stability.
- The act of seeking is therefore understood as an active, ongoing process, requiring the petitioner to turn away from distractions and maintain an unwavering focus on the establishment of God's rule within their sphere of influence. This initial step frames all subsequent requests as secondary to, yet dependent upon, this primary alignment.

Direct Communion with the Risen Savior and Lord

A significant portion of the petition is dedicated to establishing a direct, unmediated connection with the person of Jesus Christ, recognizing Him as the source of all spiritual enablement.

- The petitioner identifies Christ Jesus as the ultimate object of the search, emphasizing the desire for His presence above all else.
- The text acknowledges the transfer of spiritual power following Christ's ascension, specifically referencing the "divine spirit of the Holy Ghost whom I refer to as comforter." This establishes the Holy Spirit as the immediate conduit through

which the presence of the risen Savior is experienced in the present day.

- The request is for this Comforter to "gush into me with power and anointing," suggesting a desire for an overwhelming, unrestrained influx of divine energy, far beyond a mere trickle or subtle influence.
- The spirit of the petitioner is declared ready to receive this infusion, framing the self as a vessel prepared for divine occupation.
- The focus on the "risen savior" underscores the belief that the power being sought is resurrection power, capable of overcoming all forms of spiritual death, stagnation, or limitation within the believer's life.
- This communion is sought not just for personal comfort, but as the necessary precursor to fulfilling the mandate of authority and dominion mentioned later in the prayer.

The Impartation of the Holy Spirit and Spiritual Transformation

The prayer moves into specific demands for internal restructuring, utilizing powerful metaphors of spiritual surgery and renewal, all facilitated by the Holy Spirit.

- The central request here is for the Holy Spirit to "Perform your spiritual circumcision on my life." This concept implies a radical, internal cutting away of that which is contrary to God's will, mirroring the Old Testament covenant sign but applied spiritually to the inner being.
- The goal of this circumcision is explicitly stated as bringing about "spiritual alignment and purification within this temple." The body and spirit are viewed as a sacred temple requiring constant maintenance and cleansing.
- There is a severe decree against any impurity: "if it be anything unlike you that dwell inside me, let it be nullified, let it be cast down." This demonstrates a zero-tolerance policy for spiritual

contamination or influence that does not originate from the Divine.

- The desired outcome of this purification process is renewal and confirmation, achieved specifically "by the power of your might and spiritual atonement." This links the internal cleansing directly to the finished work of Christ on the cross.
- This transformation is not passive; it is the necessary groundwork for the next stage of the petition—the building of kingdom structures within the self.

Establishing Earthly Dominion Through Kingdom Mentality

Having established the need for internal purity and divine anointing, the petitioner articulates the desire to translate this spiritual reality into tangible authority on Earth, fulfilling what is perceived as an original mandate.

- The prayer calls for the building up of "kingdom principles and mentality." This suggests a desire to adopt the operational framework, values, and mindset of God's eternal kingdom, replacing worldly or fleshly paradigms.
- The aim is to "establish my rightful place to exercise authority and dominion upon the earth." This authority is explicitly linked back to the "original ordination upon creation for me to acquire," suggesting a desire to reclaim a lost or dormant inheritance granted at the dawn of time.
- A crucial element of this section is the recognition of spiritual warfare: "Because you have all power, allow no other powers or principalities to dominate my purpose." This acknowledges the reality of opposing spiritual forces seeking to usurp the petitioner's divinely appointed role.
- The reliance is placed entirely on divine strength to counter these forces: "but with your mighty arm, pull down each stronghold." The petitioner

recognizes their own inability to dismantle these structures alone, requiring the overwhelming, irresistible force of God's power to achieve victory over entrenched opposition.
- This theme emphasizes that spiritual seeking is intrinsically linked to practical, authoritative living, where the internal alignment manifests externally as effective dominion.

The Pursuit of Enhanced Wisdom and Unwavering Faith

The petition shifts focus to specific intellectual and volitional endowments necessary for navigating the spiritual and earthly realms effectively—wisdom and faith.

- The request is specific: "Increase my wisdom in double portions." This echoes Old Testament concepts of receiving a magnified measure of divine insight, suggesting that current wisdom levels are insufficient for the tasks ahead.
- This wisdom must be coupled with "unwavering faith for in your word which you are." The faith requested is not merely belief, but a steadfast reliance on the eternal nature of God's spoken word, recognizing that the word itself is God ("In the beginning was the word, and the word was with you").
- The text reinforces the necessity of this faith by quoting Hebrews 6:13: "but without Faith it is impossible to please him." This serves as a justification for the intensity of the request—the ability to please God is contingent upon this specific spiritual gift.
- Furthermore, the petitioner affirms the core tenets of faith required for approaching God: one must believe that God exists ("that he is") and that He actively rewards those who pursue Him diligently ("that He is a rewarder for those who diligently seek him").
- The concept of diligence is paramount here; the faith requested is not passive acceptance but an active, persistent seeking that merits

divine recompense. This section solidifies the intellectual and volitional commitment required alongside the emotional and spiritual yearning expressed earlier.

Active Engagement in Seeking God According to Prophetic Call

This section details the active steps the petitioner is taking to engage the heavens, based on a specific prophetic utterance regarding accessibility to God.

- The current petition is framed as a direct response to a heartfelt request, which is then articulated through the word of Isaiah 55:6: "Seek the LORD while he may be found; call on him while he is near." This provides a temporal urgency to the entire exercise.
- The petitioner actively engages the spiritual geography: "I call out to the Heavens above all realms of all other kingdoms that you allow to abide." This implies a recognition that multiple spiritual jurisdictions exist, but the call is directed specifically to the highest authority that permits lesser realms to exist.
- The posture adopted before this authority is one of humility and submission: "I come before your throne bowed down." This contrasts sharply with the later request for authority, showing that the reception of power must follow an act of profound reverence.
- The purpose of this humble approach is explicitly transactional in a spiritual sense: "to receive your answer, authority and power to execute this calling upon my life." The petitioner is not merely asking for blessings, but for the tools—the mandate, the strength, and the authorization—to fulfill their designated purpose.
- This theme emphasizes that seeking is an active, vocal, and geographically aware spiritual engagement that demands a tangible response from the Divine Throne.

30-day Breakthrough Prayer

The Singular, Enduring Desire for Divine Dwelling

The final scriptural anchor, Psalms 27:4, defines the ultimate, non-negotiable aspiration that underpins all the preceding requests for power, wisdom, and authority.

- The petitioner declares this desire as the "One thing have I desired of the Lord, that will I seek after." This elevates the desire for communion above all other requests for provision or power.
- The specific nature of this dwelling is defined: "that I may dwell in the house of the Lord all the days of my life." This is not a temporary visit but a permanent state of residency within God's sanctuary.
- The purpose of this lifelong dwelling is experiential: "to behold the beauty of the Lord." This speaks to an unending appreciation and contemplation of God's inherent glory and perfection.
- Furthermore, this dwelling is active and intellectual: "and to enquire in his temple." This suggests that even in perpetual presence, the relationship remains dynamic, involving ongoing learning, consultation, and revelation within the sacred space.
- All the preceding requests—for spiritual circumcision, dominion, wisdom, and power—are ultimately validated and contextualized by this final, overarching goal: ensuring that the life lived on Earth is one that leads directly and securely into eternal, intimate communion with the Divine.

The prayer serves as a comprehensive blueprint for a life wholly dedicated to seeking and manifesting the Kingdom of God. It meticulously outlines a process beginning with the absolute prioritization of God's righteousness, followed by a fervent request for direct empowerment via the Holy Spirit, leading to internal purification and spiritual alignment. The prayer then transitions to the practical application of this power, demanding the dismantling of spiritual strongholds and the establishment of ordained earthly dominion based on a kingdom mentality. Crucially, this pursuit of authority is balanced by the need for enhanced wisdom and an unwavering, active faith, acknowledging that pleasing God is impossible without it. Every request for power, authority, and spiritual endowment is ultimately tethered to the singular, overarching desire expressed in Psalms 27: 4: a lifelong, intimate dwelling within the presence of the Lord to perpetually behold His beauty and seek His counsel. The entire petition is an integrated cycle of seeking, receiving, acting, and desiring deeper communion, all grounded in the victory of the Risen Savior.

Chapter 12

My Help

My help comes from the Lord Jesus!
In quietude, I lift my gaze
To azure hills that rise and sway,
From depths of doubt, where shadows play,
My help ascends to light the maze.

The Maker of both earth and sky,
Whose hand upholds both time and grace,
Will steady me in this vast space,
His whispered strength, a gentle sigh.

Fear not, speaks the Lord; His voice is near,
I shall not be afraid of the arrows that fly by noon
He shelters me within His womb,
My enemies are scattered; He makes my path clear.

He guards my steps, my heart, my soul,
I submit unto the Lord, He guides my way,
He orders my steps so that I don't go astray
He restores my soul that my youth shall not grow old

The calling on my life has been appointed, I shall not miss
In every day, I will praise him from the east to far North Star

30-day Breakthrough Prayer

His righteous hand keeps me; He trains my hands to battle and my feet to war

In my favor the environment shifts

My miracle way maker, keeper of my gates

In the Lords hands I find my fate

Psalms 27 KJV

121 I lift up my eyes to the hills.
From where does my help come?
2 My help comes from the Lord,
who made heaven and earth.
3 He will not let your foot be moved;
he who keeps you will not slumber.
4 Behold, he who keeps Israel
will neither slumber nor sleep.
5 The Lord is your keeper;
the Lord is your shade on your right hand.
6 The sun shall not strike you by day,
nor the moon by night.
7 The Lord will keep you from all evil;
he will keep your life.
8 The Lord will keep
your going out and your coming in
from this time forth and forevermore.

Isaiah 41:10 KJV

10 fear not, for I am with you;
be not dismayed, for I am your God;
I will strengthen you, I will help you,
I will uphold you with my righteous right hand.

Amen.

30-day Breakthrough Prayer

Chapter 13

Praise And Adore

Holy is your name, Jesus

I worship and adore you

You are magnified and magnificent

Worthy omniscient

You are the Bread of Life

Gentile Redeemer having already paid the price

Marvelous of wonder, Great I am

You are the Lion and you are the lamb

Praise the risen savior, Jesus Christ is worthy to be praised

Let us exalt the King with heads bowed and arms raised

Jehovah Jireh, you will provide

Thank you in 1000 tongues do we abide

Sing unto the Lord

Give Thanksgiving and praise

I exalt your name above all other names

King of kings, you are Victorious

Lord of Lord, you are Glorious

Hallelujah!

Shout out through the Land

Hail Hail Lion of Judah, Great I Am

Comprehensive Analysis and Devotional Expansion of "Praise and Adore"

30-day Breakthrough Prayer

This prayer provides an exhaustive exploration and contextual expansion of the lyrical content found in the provided text titled "Praise and Adore." Originating from a devotional or worship context, the lyrics serve as a concise yet profound declaration of faith, focusing intensely on the attributes, titles, and worthy nature of Jesus Christ. The purpose of this extended summary is not merely to restate the brief text but to unpack the theological depth embedded within each phrase, transforming the short verses into a comprehensive meditation on divine majesty, covenant faithfulness, and the appropriate human response of worship, adoration, and exaltation. By dissecting the core themes—Holiness, Identity, Action, and Victory—this analysis aims to elaborate significantly upon the foundational expressions of praise contained within the original prayer, fulfilling the required extensive length through detailed theological and scriptural contextualization of every expressed sentiment.

The core message of "Praise and Adore" revolves around acknowledging the supreme nature of Jesus Christ and expressing active, heartfelt devotion. This section breaks down the lyrical content into its primary pillars, expanding upon the implications of each declaration.

The Acknowledgment of Divine Holiness and Worship

This theme addresses the initial calls to reverence, establishing the foundation upon which all subsequent praise is built. The lyrics begin by setting a tone of absolute sanctity and personal surrender to the divine presence.

- The Sanctity of the Name: The opening line, "Holy is your name, Jesus," immediately invokes the concept of divine separation and unmatched purity. This holiness is not merely an attribute but the very essence of the divine being, demanding reverence. In theological terms, to declare a name holy is to acknowledge its power and uniqueness, setting it apart from all earthly designations. This recognition forms the bedrock of true worship, distinguishing the Creator from the created order.

- The Posture of Personal Devotion: The immediate response to this holiness is articulated through the personal commitment: "I worship and adore you." Worship transcends mere acknowledgment; it is an active surrender of will and spirit. Adoration implies deep, affectionate reverence, suggesting an intimate relationship alongside profound respect for supreme authority. This dual action—worship (reverence for power) and adoration (love for character)—captures the comprehensive nature of the required human response to divine majesty.
- Magnificence and Incomprehensibility: The lyrics declare, "You are magnified and magnificent" and "Worthy omniscient." Magnification speaks to the endless capacity to perceive and declare His greatness, suggesting that no matter how much is said, there remains infinitely more to praise. Magnificence speaks to inherent splendor and overwhelming beauty. The attribute of omniscience—knowing all things—further solidifies the reason for this awe; the subject of worship possesses complete knowledge, making His decrees absolute and His wisdom unparalleled.
- The Paradox of the Great I Am: The declaration "Great I am" is a direct echo of the divine self-revelation to Moses (Exodus 3:14). This title signifies eternal, self-existent being—a reality that requires no external validation or definition. It is the ultimate statement of sovereignty, implying that Jesus is the source and sustainer of all existence, a concept that inherently dwarfs human comprehension and necessitates profound awe.

The Multifaceted Identity and Roles of Christ

The lyrics move from abstract attributes to specific, relational titles that define Jesus's role in salvation history and ongoing spiritual life. These titles reveal the comprehensive nature of His identity.

- The Duality of the Lamb and the Lion: The phrase "You are the Lion and the lamb" encapsulates a central biblical paradox of Christ. The Lion of Judah represents unconquerable strength, royal authority, and fierce justice. Conversely, the Lamb symbolizes sacrificial innocence, meekness, and substitutionary atonement. To praise both simultaneously is to acknowledge that the same being who possesses ultimate power willingly submitted to ultimate vulnerability for the sake of redemption. This duality is crucial for a complete understanding of the Savior.
- The Triumph of the Risen Savior: The text celebrates, "Praise the risen savior, Jesus Christ is worthy to be praised." The resurrection is the linchpin of Christian faith. Praising the "risen savior" emphasizes victory over death and the validation of His sacrifice. Worthiness here is directly tied to the successful completion of the redemptive work, confirming His authority to receive all honor.
- The Posture of Submission in Exaltation: The call, "Let us exalt the King with heads bowed and arms raised," describes the physical manifestation of worship. Bowed heads signify humility, submission, and recognition of the King's authority. Raised arms signify acceptance, surrender, and openness to receive blessing or power. This physical posture illustrates the necessary internal state: reverence coupled with active reception.
- The Covenant Provider: Jehovah Jireh: The specific invocation, "Jehovah Jireh, you will provide," anchors the praise in the covenant relationship. Jehovah Jireh (The Lord Will Provide) recalls Abraham's testimony, assuring the worshipper that divine provision is guaranteed. This moves the focus from abstract majesty to tangible, daily care and sustenance,

emphasizing God's faithfulness in meeting human needs.

The Expression of Perpetual and Universal Praise

This theme focuses on the required manner and scope of the human response—how often and how widely this adoration should be expressed.

- The Inadequacy of Human Language: The line, "Thank you in 1000 tongues do we abide," highlights the insufficiency of human expression to capture divine glory. The reference to a thousand tongues suggests an impossible, overwhelming multitude of ways to give thanks, implying that even the most eloquent and varied praise falls short. Abiding in this thankfulness suggests a continuous state of gratitude rather than a momentary feeling.
- Mandates for Active Worship: Several lines function as direct commands or invitations to worship: "Sing unto the Lord" and "Give Thanksgiving and praise." Singing is an active, audible form of worship that engages the spirit, mind, and voice. Thanksgiving is the acknowledgment of benefits received, while praise is the celebration of inherent goodness, making these actions inseparable components of devotion.
- Supremacy in Naming: The declaration, "I exalt your name above all other names," directly references the scriptural mandate that every knee should bow and every tongue confess that Jesus is Lord (Philippians 2:9-11). This is a declaration of ultimate supremacy, asserting that no earthly title, philosophy, or deity can stand equal to or above the name of Jesus. Exaltation here means lifting the name to the highest possible position in the hierarchy of all things known or unknown.
- Broadcasting the Message: The instruction, "Shout out through the Land," demands that praise be public, unrestrained, and geographically widespread. Worship is not intended to be a private affair but a proclamation that

permeates the entire sphere of influence, ensuring the message of Christ's worth is heard across all boundaries.

Declarations of Sovereign Victory and Kingship

The final cluster focuses on Christ's established dominion and ultimate triumph over all opposition, reinforcing the reasons for the preceding adoration.

- The Reigning Monarchs: The lyrics identify Christ through His supreme royal titles: "King of kings, you are Victorious" and "Lord of Lord, you are Glorious." These titles denote hierarchical superiority over all earthly and spiritual rulers. Victory is not a potential outcome but an established fact, secured through His life, death, and resurrection. Glory is the inherent radiance and majesty that accompanies this undisputed reign.
- The Ultimate Acclamation: The simple yet powerful interjection, "Hallelujah!" serves as the ultimate expression of praise, meaning "Praise Yah (God)." It is a universal, timeless cry of joy and affirmation that encapsulates all the preceding declarations of worthiness and victory. It is the spontaneous overflow of a heart overwhelmed by the greatness described.
- The Final, Definitive Title: The closing invocation, "Hail Hail Lion of Judah," returns to a powerful Old Testament reference, linking Jesus directly to the messianic lineage promised to the tribe of Judah. Hail signifies a formal greeting of respect and allegiance to a sovereign ruler. By identifying Him as the Lion of Judah, the lyrics affirm His legitimate claim to the throne and His ultimate conquering power, serving as the final, resounding affirmation of His identity as the triumphant Messiah.

Deep Theological Elaboration on Divine Attributes and Worship

The initial lines of "Praise and Adore" establish a framework for understanding the object of worship—a being whose nature necessitates absolute reverence. This section expands upon the concepts of holiness, magnificence, and omniscience as presented in the lyrics.

- The Profound Meaning of Holiness: When the lyrics state, "Holy is your name, Jesus," they invoke the Hebrew concept of Qadosh, meaning set apart, consecrated, or utterly distinct. To worship a holy being requires a corresponding purification of the worshipper. The magnitude of this holiness implies that every action, thought, and attribute of Jesus is perfectly aligned with divine perfection, rendering Him utterly incapable of error or compromise. This inherent holiness is the primary reason for the subsequent declaration of worship. The act of worship, therefore, is an attempt, however flawed, to mirror that set-off nature by dedicating one's own life and focus exclusively to the divine source.
- "You are magnified and magnificent," requires careful distinction. Magnification is an active verb applied to the subject; it is the process by which the worshipper continually increases the perceived stature of Christ in their own mind and in the public sphere. It suggests that the true scope of His greatness is so vast that it must be perpetually enlarged in our perception to keep pace with reality. Magnificence, conversely, is an inherent quality—the inherent splendor, grandeur, and awe-inspiring beauty resident within Him. It is the visible manifestation of His glory. A being that is both inherently magnificent and offers devotion. This concept prevents worship from ever becoming stagnant; there is always a new facet of glory to behold and declare.
- Omniscience as the Basis for Trust: The attribute "Worthy omniscient" connects knowledge directly to worthiness. Omniscience means total, complete, and perfect knowledge of all things past, present, and future. This attribute underpins the

worshipper's ability to trust implicitly. If Jesus is omniscient, then His guidance is infallible, His judgment is just, and His plans are perfect. This knowledge extends to the deepest recesses of the human heart, meaning that the worship offered is seen and understood in its true intent, not just its outward form. This comprehensive knowledge justifies the surrender implied in the following lines of adoration.

- The Eternal Self-Definition: Great I Am: The phrase "Great I am" is perhaps the most potent statement of identity. It is the affirmation of self-sufficiency. Unlike created beings who exist contingently, Jesus exists necessarily. This title confirms His pre-existence and His role as the ultimate reality. When the worshipper acknowledges this, they are recognizing that their own existence and purpose are derived entirely from this eternal source. The greatness is not merely comparative (greater than others) but absolute (the standard of greatness itself). This recognition naturally leads to the next identification, which bridges the eternal nature with the historical mission.

Expansion on Christ’s Redemptive Titles and Historical Significance

The lyrics transition to identifying Jesus through His specific actions and roles within the narrative of salvation, emphasizing both His sacrificial nature and His ultimate authority.

- The Paradox of the Lion and the Lamb: This pairing is central to understanding the atonement. The Lamb speaks of substitutionary sacrifice—taking the penalty for sin upon Himself. This requires immense humility and love. The Lion speaks of the power required to overcome the penalty of death and the forces of darkness. The worthiness of Christ stems from the fact that the one who possessed the absolute power (the Lion) chose the path of ultimate weakness (the Lamb) to achieve redemption. To worship the Lion/Lamb is to honor both the cost of salvation and the power that made that cost effective.

- The Triumph of the Risen Savior: The emphasis on the "risen savior" is critical. Praise is directed not merely to the historical figure who died, but to the conquering Lord who lives eternally. The worthiness mentioned is intrinsically linked to the resurrection, which serves as the divine receipt confirming that the sacrifice was accepted and the victory over death secured. This reality transforms worship from a memorial service into a celebration of ongoing, active salvation.
- The Covenant Relationship and Provision: The invocation of "Jehovah Jireh" grounds the abstract praise in practical faith. This title assures the believer that the omniscient, magnificent King is also intimately concerned with their earthly well-being. Provision encompasses spiritual needs (grace, forgiveness) and physical needs (sustenance, guidance). The assurance that "you will provide" establishes a foundation of security, allowing the worshipper to approach the majestic King without fear, knowing that His majesty is coupled with paternal care.
- The Necessity of Physical and Vocal Response: The instruction to exalt the King "with heads bowed and arms raised" outlines a holistic worship experience. The bowing head is an act of submission, acknowledging the King's absolute right to rule over the individual will. The raised arms are often interpreted as an act of surrender, reception, or expectant praise. This physical embodiment ensures that the internal spiritual reality is expressed outwardly, making the worship complete and visible. Furthermore, the call to "Sing unto the Lord" mandates the use of the voice—the most personal and immediate tool of human expression—to convey gratitude and adoration, ensuring the praise is dynamic and audible.

30-day Breakthrough Prayer

The Scope and Intensity of Perpetual Gratitude

The lyrics demand that the response of the heart be translated into continuous, expansive action, moving beyond mere feeling into sustained lifestyle.

- The Limitless Nature of Thanksgiving: The acknowledgment, "Thank you in 1000 tongues do we abide," is a hyperbolic expression signifying that human language is inherently limited when attempting to quantify gratitude owed to God. The desire to use a thousand tongues suggests a yearning for infinite expression. To "abide" in this thankfulness means that gratitude is not a fleeting emotion triggered by a blessing, but a constant state of being—the default setting of the soul in the presence of the Savior. This constant state of thankfulness is the prerequisite for receiving further grace.
- Exaltation Above All Authority: The declaration, "I exalt your name above all other names," is a definitive statement of priority. In a world filled with competing loyalties, authorities, and philosophies, this line establishes an unwavering hierarchy. Every other concept—personal ambition, earthly power, societal expectation—is deliberately placed beneath the singular, supreme name of Jesus. This act of exalting is an ongoing commitment to prioritizing the divine reputation above all else, ensuring that in every decision, His name is held in the highest esteem.
- The Reign of the Victorious King: The titles "King of kings" and "Lord of Lord" are superlative affirmations of sovereignty. They place Jesus above every conceivable earthly monarch, political structure, and even the hierarchy of spiritual beings. The accompanying descriptor, "you are Victorious," confirms that this kingship is not merely theoretical but actively demonstrated through conquest over sin, death, and the adversary. This victory is the source of the worshipper's hope and the justification for the ensuing "Glorious" acknowledgment. The glory is

the visible manifestation of this established, victorious reign.

- The Unrestrained Proclamation: The command to "Shout out through the Land" transforms worship into evangelism. Praise is not meant to be contained within the walls of a sanctuary; it must be broadcast widely. Shouting implies urgency, conviction, and volume, ensuring that the message of Christ's worthiness penetrates all geographical and social boundaries. This public declaration is the ultimate fulfillment of the internal adoration—the heart's deepest conviction made manifest to the world.

The lyrics of "Praise and Adore," though brief, function as a comprehensive theological roadmap for worship. The key takeaway is the absolute necessity of aligning one's entire being—intellectually, emotionally, and physically—with the revealed nature of Jesus Christ. The prayer establishes that Jesus is worthy because of His inherent holiness, His self-existent nature ("Great I Am"), and His comprehensive identity encompassing both sacrificial love (the Lamb) and conquering power (the Lion). The required human response is multifaceted: active worship and adoration, perpetual thanksgiving expressed through every available means ("1000 tongues"), and the public, unrestrained proclamation of His supreme authority ("Shout out through the Land"). Ultimately, the text culminates in the affirmation of His established dominion as the Victorious King of Kings and Lord of Lords, whose name must be exalted above all others, providing an inexhaustible foundation for eternal praise and adoration. The entire composition serves as a powerful, concise liturgy demanding total devotion based on the undeniable reality of Christ's divine majesty and redemptive accomplishment.

30-day Breakthrough Prayer

Chapter 14

Fearful and Wonderful

Psalm 139:14

[14] I praise you because I am fearfully and wonderfully made;
your works are wonderful,

Job 28:28

[28] And he said to the human race,
"The fear of the Lord—that is wisdom,
and to shun evil is understanding."

Great and Merciful Father, It is actualization that your limits are boundless, all knowing and all-encompassing and therefore in reverence, I commence to your word. There are none other than you shall, I fear. You said that the fear of the Lord is wisdom, I will not be fearful of man because nothing can happen without your authority in my life. It is you who bring righteousness. It is you who deliver. It is you who can destroy. In you I abide. I come before my creator bowed in head so that you can build me as the architect of my soul. I come in expectancy that you are kind and merciful. I come in faith that what has already been established on earth will also be established in heaven. It is with man did you perform a perfect work, not craftiness for destruction. You use your right arm to defend, and none can stand against you.

You have fed the multitude and led the captives out of captivity. Show me your wonder. Do a mighty work and show your humble servant favor.

A Comprehensive Exposition on Divine Awe, Wisdom, and Supplication

This prayer presents a profound meditation rooted in scriptural foundations and expressed through personal, devotional prayer. Its core purpose is to articulate a worldview centered on the absolute sovereignty, boundless knowledge, and merciful nature of the Creator. The text moves systematically from acknowledging the inherent wonder of human creation to establishing the proper posture of reverence—the fear of the Lord—as the sole source of wisdom. It functions as a declaration of dependence, where the speaker rejects fear of temporal powers in favor of abiding in the one who establishes righteousness, delivers, and defends. Ultimately, the prayer culminates in a heartfelt petition for the manifestation of God's power, asking for visible wonders and favor bestowed upon a humble servant.

The opening segment establishes a foundational truth regarding the speaker's existence, drawn directly from Psalm 139:14, which serves as the initial anchor for the subsequent prayer and reflection.

- The Dual Nature of Creation: The declaration that one is "fearfully and wonderfully made" is explored not merely as a statement of biological fact, but as a theological recognition of divine artistry. The term "fearfully" implies a sense of overwhelming awe and perhaps even trepidation when contemplating the complexity and intricacy woven into human being by an infinite Creator. This is not fear of harm, but fear of the sublime.
- The Wonder of Divine Design: Complementing the awe is the element of "wonderfully made." This speaks to the intentionality, beauty, and perfect suitability of the design for its intended purpose. Every aspect of the self is thus viewed as a testament to God's meticulous planning, far surpassing human comprehension or imitation.
- The Scope of God's Works: The text broadens this personal observation to encompass all of God's creative endeavors, stating simply that "your works are wonderful." This suggests that the same meticulous, awe-inspiring power evident in the

individual is present in the entirety of creation, reinforcing the boundless nature of the divine architect mentioned later in the prayer. The recognition of this wonder compels the speaker toward reverence.

The Foundation of True Knowledge: Fear and Understanding

The transition to Job 28:28 introduces the essential prerequisite for engaging with the divine reality: the correct orientation of the heart toward the Creator, defining wisdom and understanding in spiritual terms.

- Defining Wisdom through Reverence: The text highlights the assertion that "The fear of the Lord—that is wisdom." This wisdom is presented as the highest form of knowledge, achievable only through a profound respect and submission to God's authority. It is the recognition of divine majesty that unlocks true insight into existence.
- Understanding as Active Avoidance: Wisdom is paired with understanding, defined as "to shun evil." This implies that true comprehension of God's nature is not passive intellectual assent but active moral commitment. Understanding manifests practically by deliberately turning away from that which opposes the divine will.
- The Inseparability of Awe and Action: The scriptural citation frames the entire devotional exercise that follows. If wisdom is the fear of the Lord, then the prayer offered must necessarily be one of humility and submission, recognizing that the speaker approaches a being whose very nature demands awe.

Acknowledging Divine Sovereignty and Boundless Limits

- God's limits are "boundless, all knowing and all encompassing."
- "There are none other than you shall I fear." This establishes a hierarchy of authority.

- "Nothing can happen without your authority in my life." This belief removes the possibility of random misfortune, placing all circumstances—good or ill—under the umbrella of divine permission and ultimate purpose.

The Rejection of Earthly Fear and Reliance on Divine Authority

- "I will not be fearful of man," is a direct consequence of the preceding theological assertions. If God controls all outcomes, then the judgment or actions of other humans hold no ultimate power over the speaker's spiritual standing or destiny.
- "It is you who bring righteousness." This is not merely an abstract concept but an active provision from the divine source.
- "It is you who deliver. It is you who can destroy." This acknowledges God's capacity for both salvation and judgment, reinforcing why He alone deserves ultimate allegiance.
- "In you I abide." This signifies a continuous state of reliance, dwelling within the sphere of God's established order and protection.

Posture of Humility and Spiritual Rebuilding

The prayer shifts focus from defining God's attributes to defining the speaker's necessary internal state for receiving divine interaction, emphasizing transformation and expectation.

- Bowing Before the Creator: The speaker approaches God "bowed in spirit." This physical metaphor represents total surrender, humility, and the cessation of self-reliance or pride. It is the prerequisite for spiritual construction.
- The Divine Architect of the Soul: The request is for God to "build me as the architect of my soul." This is a plea for sanctification—a process where the divine will actively shapes the

inner being, replacing flawed human design with perfect divine structure. The speaker recognizes that true self-improvement requires divine blueprints.

- Expectancy and Faith in Mercy: The approach is characterized by two positive attitudes: "expectancy that you are kind and merciful," and "faith that what has already been established on earth will also be established in heaven." This links present spiritual hope with eternal certainty, trusting that divine decrees are consistent across realms.
- The Perfection of Divine Action: A clear distinction is drawn between divine methodology and human fallibility: "It is with man did you perform a perfect work, not craftiness for destruction." God's intervention is characterized by flawless execution aimed at positive creation, contrasting sharply with the deceptive or destructive nature often found in human endeavors.
- Unassailable Defense: The power of God's defense is emphasized through the imagery of the "right arm," signifying immediate, mighty, and irresistible strength: "You use your right arm to defend, and none can stand against you." This reinforces the earlier point about the futility of fearing human opposition.

Recalling Acts of Deliverance and Petition for Manifestation

The final section of the prayer grounds the current request in historical precedent—God's proven ability to intervene dramatically on behalf of His people—before issuing a final, earnest plea for visible demonstration.

- Precedent of Mighty Intervention: The speaker recalls monumental acts of divine provision and liberation: God "fed the multitude and led the captives out of captivity." These examples serve as evidence that God is not merely a distant sovereign but an active agent of miraculous provision and liberation.

- The Call for Visible Wonder: Based on this history, the speaker issues a direct command rooted in faith: "Show me your wonder." This is a request for an experience that transcends the ordinary, a direct encounter with the marvelous aspects of God's power.
- The Demand for Mighty Work: Following the request for wonder is the petition for a "mighty work." This suggests a need for an undeniable demonstration of power in the present circumstances of the speaker's life or community, something that cannot be explained away by natural means.
- Favor for the Humble Servant: The entire devotional exercise concludes with a request for personal blessing contingent upon the speaker's acknowledged humility: "Do a mighty work and show your humble servant favor." This final appeal ties the demonstration of divine power directly to the posture of submission adopted throughout the preceding meditation.

The document, structured around scriptural citation and heartfelt supplication, functions as a comprehensive theological statement on proper relationship with the divine. The key takeaways revolve around the inherent majesty of creation ("fearfully and wonderfully made"), the necessity of reverence ("the fear of the Lord") as the sole path to wisdom, and the absolute sovereignty of God over all events. The speaker resolves to live free from earthly fear, recognizing that divine authority governs all reality, and commits to abiding in that reality. The prayer is a disciplined exercise in aligning the inner spirit—bowing before the Creator to be rebuilt—with the external reality of God's perfect, defending power. The ultimate finding is that a life lived in awe and submission naturally leads to the expectation and petition for visible, mighty works and the bestowal of divine favor upon the humble believer.

Chapter 15

Graciously Restored

How gracious is the love you bestow, Father in Heaven and above the earth. You have given your begotten son as the atonement of an evil humanity; that those who look upon you with a repentance heart believing that Jesus Christ is Lord will be saved. Great by your works have you given us power to overcome the evil one. You have considered us with grace and mercy into the everlasting. You are a God whose grace provides accomplishments and with a sincere heart I give you thanks. I thank you that you have given to the undeserving, you have given to the weak, you have given to the poor, you have given to us that sin may be dead.

Let there be restoration to those who ask. I am asking for your restoration in all measures of my shortcomings, rather it be spiritual, physical or things that tarnish. Rebuild my entirety of stature, heart, and soul that my pillars of stature cannot be destroyed by man, nor the evil one that contaminates the life of man.

I call in alignment that you can and will rebuild me. That you are releasing all the necessary equipment thus in spirit, truth and substance that constitute your blessings upon my life, my faith, my family, my church, my business, my loved ones, my government, my environment and community that blessings shall follow this prayer, and that blessings are being released to me. I call upon the Heavens to give quick relief to all the needed areas to perform vital, essential and numerous restoration to sub stain and equip that my equity has gained a surplus in value, my spirit overfloweth, new life and youth overfloweth, the wealth of the righteous overfloweth, protection and prosperity overfloweth; all these that I ask or need has the power and ability to surplus and bring increase; now unto Him who is able to do exceedingly and abundantly, to Jesus be the Christ in whose names these works shall be performed.

30-day Breakthrough Prayer

It is you and only you, God the Father, Son and Holy Spirit who holds the key to both the Heaven and hell to perform and ordain these works, that no evil intentions shall interrupt that goodness shall be fulfilled in my life. Send your angelic host of angels that they shall cancel and destroy the works of darkness and anything or anyone assigned to frustrate the purpose of my life or loved ones that we are whole and there are unity, discipline and order in my house and gates.

I speak those things that are not as if they are to bring into existence and perfect alignment with you Lord Jesus, with divine authority to put on and cast down all things that are prudence. I speak in authority to devour the blacklist, I sever rejections, denials and decline off my account and my name by the power of the blood, I am consecrated and approved of what is Royal, noble and just. This is my dew season to reap the harvest that has been stored up for me. There will be no denying me of the plenty, good and just rewards on the earth. I misalign the branches of greed, evil and poverty that Him who sits in judgement may reap their rewards according to their own work, their own deeds. There are none that sit above your throne. Those who seek to bring injustice or withhold the harvest that you have given to me will be punished by my God. Disentangle the cords of the righteous and unrighteousness to pour out your favor amongst the people who are called according to your purpose that no scheme nor famine shall enter their gates. Show us your grace and mercy, give us restoration in the kingdom of systems that we shall be first and not last. Gates be ye opened. I will be sure to give you all the glory and honor. I seal this prayer by the blood of Jesus in the book of the volume that is written of us. We shall prevail, we shall win, we shall persevere with success, opportunity, new inventions, technology, opposition is defeated and grants and lending has fallen upon your people that we are investors, and prosperity is upon us.

In Jesus name.

Amen.

Graciously Restored: A Declaration of Divine Restoration and Overflow

This prayer is a profound and detailed spiritual declaration, structured as a prayer, centered on themes of gratitude, personal restoration, the assertion of divine authority, and the expectation of abundant blessings and victory over adversity. The core purpose is to align the petitioner's life—spiritually, physically, and materially—with the will and grace of God, specifically invoking the power inherent in the atonement of Jesus Christ. It moves sequentially from acknowledging God's mercy and the gift of salvation to specific demands for rebuilding, the release of necessary spiritual resources, the declaration of overflowing prosperity, and finally, the authoritative sealing of these declarations against all forms of darkness and opposition, culminating in a firm expectation of prevailing success in all endeavors.

I. Profound Gratitude for Divine Love and Atonement

The foundation of this declaration rests upon an overwhelming expression of thanks for the boundless and gracious love bestowed by the Father in Heaven. This gratitude is deeply rooted in the understanding of the ultimate sacrifice made for humanity's failings.

- The petitioner expresses deep thankfulness for the provision of God's begotten Son, Jesus Christ, who served as the necessary atonement for the inherent evil of humanity. This act of grace is recognized as the sole means by which those who approach God with a repentant heart and believe that Jesus Christ is Lord can achieve salvation.

- Acknowledgement is given to the great works of God, which have furnished the petitioner with the requisite power to successfully overcome the influence and actions of the evil one. This recognition emphasizes a reliance on divine strength rather than personal capability in the spiritual battle.
- The prayer highlights the consideration shown by God, who has extended grace and mercy toward the petitioner, ensuring their place in the everlasting. This grace is not merely a passive gift but an active force that provides accomplishments and tangible results in the life of the believer.
- A sincere heart is offered in thanksgiving for the distribution of these blessings to those who are deemed undeserving. Specific mention is made of the provision extended to the weak, the poor, and the generally overlooked, all for the ultimate purpose that sin might be rendered inoperative and ultimately cease to have dominion.
- The petitioner emphasizes that this divine love is characterized by its impartiality and generosity, extending favor where it was not earned, thereby setting the stage for the subsequent requests for restoration based on this established foundation of undeserved grace.

II. The Earnest Petition for Comprehensive Personal Restoration

Following the expression of thanks, the prayer shifts into a focused, urgent petition for complete restoration across every aspect of the petitioner's being and circumstances.

- A direct request is made for restoration in "all measures" concerning personal shortcomings, encompassing spiritual deficiencies, physical ailments, and any aspects of life or character that have become tarnished or diminished over time.

- The prayer calls for a complete rebuilding of the petitioner's entirety, specifically targeting the stature, the heart, and the soul. This rebuilding is sought with the intent that the resulting spiritual and personal pillars of stature become impregnable, incapable of being destroyed or dismantled by human interference or the corrupting influence of the evil one that seeks to contaminate human life.
- The petitioner actively calls into alignment the power and will of God to execute this rebuilding process. This is not a passive hope but an active invocation, demanding that God releases all the necessary components required for this transformation.
- This necessary "equipment" is defined broadly, encompassing elements in spirit, truth, and substance, all of which are essential constituents of God's blessings intended for the petitioner's life. The scope of this requested restoration covers the entirety of the individual's sphere of influence and being.

III. Calling Forth Spiritual Equipment and Blessings for Life Domains

The scope of the requested restoration is explicitly detailed across numerous critical domains of the petitioner's existence, demanding that blessings follow this prayer and be actively released from the Heavens.

- The prayer itemizes the specific areas requiring immediate and vital restoration: the petitioner's personal faith, their immediate family unit, their involvement in the church, their business endeavors, their relationships with loved ones, their engagement with government structures, and their surrounding environment and community.
- The petitioner calls upon the Heavens to grant "quick relief" to all these identified areas, ensuring the provision of essential and numerous restorations necessary to sustain and equip the individual.

- This restoration is expected to yield tangible spiritual and material results, specifically ensuring that the petitioner's equity gains a surplus in value, moving beyond mere sufficiency to abundance.
- The declaration anticipates a state where the spirit overflows, where new life and youth are continually renewed and overflowing, and crucially, where the wealth associated with the righteous is also in a state of overflow.
- Furthermore, the declaration demands an overflow of protection and prosperity. All these requested elements—the ability to surplus and bring increase—are acknowledged as being powered by the divine entity capable of doing "exceedingly and abundantly, "specifically naming Jesus the Christ as the conduit through which these works shall be performed.

IV. Declaration of Overflow, Surplus Value, and Righteous Prosperity

This section focuses on articulating the expected outcome of the divine intervention, moving from petition to authoritative declaration of an abundant state.

- The central theme is the establishment of surplus value in the petitioner's equity, signifying a state where resources and spiritual capital exceed what is required for basic sustenance or expectation.
- The spiritual condition is described as one of perpetual overflow, where the spirit is not merely content but actively brimming with divine energy and life force. This spiritual overflow is intrinsically linked to the physical and temporal blessings received.
- The declaration specifically calls for the overflow of the "wealth of the righteous," positioning the petitioner within a category entitled to specific, divinely sanctioned material abundance.

- Protection is demanded as a constant state, ensuring that the prosperity being established is secured against external threats. This prosperity is not accidental but ordained, possessing the inherent power and ability to continuously surplus and generate further increase.
- The petitioner firmly attributes the source of this power and ability to the one who can perform beyond all measure—Jesus the Christ—under whose name these powerful works of restoration and increase are commanded to manifest.

V. Invocation of the Trinity and Command for Angelic Protection

The declaration solidifies its authority by recognizing the singular, ultimate power structure governing existence and demands active intervention from the heavenly host to secure the declared blessings.

- The petitioner explicitly acknowledges that the Father, Son, and Holy Spirit are the sole entities holding the keys to both Heaven and Hell, granting them the exclusive authority to perform and ordain these requested works of restoration and blessing.
- A crucial protective clause is invoked: that no evil intentions, whether originating from earthly or spiritual sources, shall be permitted to interrupt the fulfillment of the goodness declared in this prayer within the petitioner's life.
- A direct command is issued for the deployment of the "angelic host of angels." These celestial forces are tasked with a specific mission: to immediately cancel and destroy any works of darkness that have been established against the petitioner or their loved ones.
- This angelic mandate extends to neutralizing any person or entity assigned with the purpose of frustrating the divine purpose set forth for the petitioner's life. The desired outcome is a state of wholeness, unity, discipline, and established order within the petitioner's "house and gates,"

signifying complete domestic and personal sovereignty.

VI. Exercising Divine Authority to Speak Things into Existence

The second page shifts the focus toward the active, authoritative voice of the petitioner, utilizing spiritual power to shape reality in alignment with the divine will.

- The petitioner speaks forth things that are currently absent or unrealized, commanding them to come into existence as if they already are, thereby achieving a "perfect alignment" with Lord Jesus.
- This speech is backed by "divine authority," which is asserted with the power to both establish (put on) and dismantle (cast down) all things that contradict the established divine prudence and plan.
- Specific negative structures are targeted for immediate dissolution: the petitioner speaks with authority to "devour the blacklist," effectively erasing any negative records or designations against them.
- Furthermore, the petitioner severs all forms of rejection, denial, and decline that may have been attached to their account or name, explicitly invoking the binding and cleansing power of the blood of Jesus Christ for this separation.
- The petitioner declares themselves consecrated and approved, affirming their identity as possessing what is "Royal, noble and just," setting a high standard for their current reality.

VII. Severing Negative Attachments and Claiming Stored Harvest

This section emphasizes the timing of the blessing—the "dew season"—and the right to reap rewards that have been accumulated over time but previously inaccessible.

- The current period is identified as the petitioner's "dew season," a time specifically designated for reaping the harvest that has been stored up on their behalf. This implies a period of overdue reward and abundance coming to fruition.
- The declaration asserts that there will be no legitimate denial of the "plenty, good and just rewards" that are due to the petitioner on the earth, signifying material and experiential fulfillment.
- The petitioner actively works to misalign negative spiritual or structural branches, specifically naming greed, evil, and poverty, commanding that these elements be separated from the petitioner's sphere.
- This misalignment is intended to ensure that those who sit in judgment—those who operate outside of divine alignment—will reap their rewards strictly according to their own works and deeds, without affecting the petitioner.
- A powerful statement of divine sovereignty is made there are none who possess authority above God's throne. Consequently, any entity seeking to impose injustice or withhold the harvest divinely granted to the petitioner will face punishment directly from God.

VIII. Asserting Divine Judgment Against Injustice and Evil Structures

The declaration continues to assert divine oversight and the consequences for those who attempt to obstruct the flow of blessings.

- The petitioner calls for the disentanglement of cords representing both righteousness and unrighteousness, seeking a clear pathway for divine favor to be poured out universally among those who are called according to God's true purpose.
- This clarity is sought so that no scheme, conspiracy, or famine—whether spiritual or

material—is permitted to enter the gates of the petitioner's domain.

- The prayer appeals for a manifestation of God's grace and mercy, coupled with a specific request for restoration within the "kingdom of systems." This implies a desire for structural realignment so that the petitioner and their people shall occupy the position of being first, rather than lagging behind as last.
- The command is issued for the gates to be opened, symbolizing the removal of all barriers to access and manifestation. The petitioner commits to ensuring that all glory and honor for these manifestations are returned solely to God.

IX. Seeking Systemic Restoration and Primacy Through Grace

The focus here is on establishing a new order within established systems, ensuring that the petitioner's group achieves a position of leadership and priority.

- The petitioner solidifies the entire prayer by sealing it through the potent authority of the blood of Jesus, linking these declarations to the immutable record written in the "book of the volume" concerning them.
- A confident affirmation of future success is made: "We shall prevail, we shall win, we shall persevere with success." This perseverance is linked directly to tangible outcomes such as opportunity, the arrival of new inventions, and advancements in technology.
- The declaration asserts the defeat of all opposition, stating clearly that resistance is overcome. Furthermore, it anticipates the arrival of financial support in the form of grants and lending falling upon the people.
- This financial influx is intended to transform the status of the people, establishing them firmly as investors within the economic and spiritual landscape. The ultimate state declared

is that prosperity is actively upon them, marking a definitive shift in their material reality.

X. Sealing the Covenant and Declaring Ultimate Prevailing Success

The final moments of the declaration serve to finalize the spiritual transaction, invoking the authority of Jesus' name to ensure the execution of all preceding petitions.

- The entire body of requests and declarations is formally sealed by invoking the power inherent in the name of Jesus the Christ, confirming that these works are established and irreversible.
- The expectation is absolute victory across all fronts—prevailing, winning, and succeeding through perseverance. This success is not limited to spiritual endurance but includes tangible gains like opportunity and innovation.
- The prayer concludes with a final, powerful statement of assured outcome: opposition is definitively defeated, and financial resources (grants and lending) are now flowing toward the people, positioning them as active investors.
- The final word is a declaration that prosperity is not merely hoped for but is actively present upon the people, solidifying the transition from petition to realized state. The prayer concludes with the formal closing, "In Jesus name. Amen."

The prayer "Graciously Restored" functions as a spiritual blueprint for transformation, built upon a foundation of deep gratitude for divine mercy and the redemptive work of Jesus Christ. It moves from acknowledging past grace to demanding comprehensive restoration across spiritual, physical, and material domains. The core takeaway is the petitioner's active assertion of divine authority—speaking things into existence, severing negative attachments like blacklists and rejections, and commanding the release of stored blessings. The prayer culminates in a powerful declaration of systemic victory, where opposition is defeated, new opportunities arise, and the community is established in a state of overflowing wealth, protection, and primacy, all sealed and guaranteed by the authority of the Trinity and the blood of Jesus. The entire text is a forceful, detailed expectation of abundance and order replacing all forms of lack and chaos.

Chapter 16

Anointed and Appointed

Isaiah 54:17

No weapon formed against me shall prosper

Let the divine appointment in the Heavenly realm shine upon the earth to anoint my purpose with purpose and leadership, let the Anointed One have favor on me and show his great mercy to strengthen my life with power and triumph over my enemies, let the favor of Moses, Joshua, Daniel, Esther, Ruth and David come upon me that the Lord look upon me in the earth and deliver me from them that pursue me. Many obstacles stood in accountancy to dismantle my purpose, let them be put to shame who seek to destroy me and tarnish my life with doubt, fear, idleness, poverty and death. I cancel Satan's plan to steal, kill and destroy my life. I rebuke the devil and his children any authority to destroy my future. Systems break and bend when used to subdue me unjust. They are restricted from operating and exercising authority over my property, destiny, my soul, children and grandchildren, family and friends. Give angels charge over me to ordain my destiny with love, greatness, long life, goodness and mercy. I have a fresh anointing to prosper upon the earth. I am blessed and more than a conquer who can do all things in Christ Jesus with no setbacks, set ups or mishaps. No giant can defeat me. The army of the Lord keeps watch over me, avenge my enemies. Limitations and restrictions are broken off my life! Chains are broken off my life! Remove jealousy and envy, hatred, monitoring spirits, witchcraft, evil intentions, sorcery and theft far from me. God is blessing me with good health, wealth, peace, love, happiness, purpose and authority to execute my destiny on the earth. My prayers are not Earthbound but are ascended into the heavens that whatever I shall bind upon the earth shall also be bound into the Heavens. In Jesus name bring it to pass.

Amen.

Psalms 91 KJV

91 He who dwells in the shelter of the Most High
will abide in the shadow of the Almighty.
2 I will say[a] to the Lord, "My refuge and
my fortress,
my God, in whom I trust."
3 For he will deliver you from the snare of the
fowler
and from the deadly pestilence.
4 He will cover you with his pinions,
and under his wings you will find refuge;
his faithfulness is a shield and buckler.
5 You will not fear the terror of the night,
nor the arrow that flies by day,
6 nor the pestilence that stalks in darkness,
nor the destruction that wastes at noonday.
7 A thousand may fall at your side,
ten thousand at your right hand,
but it will not come near you.
8 You will only look with your eyes
and see the recompense of the wicked.
9 Because you have made the Lord your dwelling
place—
the Most High, who is my refuge[b]—
10 no evil shall be allowed to befall you,
no plague come near your tent.
11 For he will command his angels concerning you
to guard you in all your ways.
12 On their hands they will bear you up,
lest you strike your foot against a stone.
13 You will tread on the lion and the adder;
the young lion and the serpent you will trample
underfoot.
14 "Because he holds fast to me in love, I will
deliver him;
I will protect him, because he knows my name.
15 When he calls to me, I will answer him;
I will be with him in trouble;
I will rescue him and honor him.

16 With long life I will satisfy him
and show him my salvation."

30-day Breakthrough Prayer

Chapter 17

Your Mighty Arm

Mighty is the arm of God. No one can stand against you. Use your sovereign power to deliver, save and defend us. Out stretch your arm to save me from those who seek to overtake me. Scatter them that are proud. Jeremiah 32:17 "Oh, Lord God! You have made the heavens in the Earth by your great power and outstretched arm nothing is too hard for you.

Exodus 6:6" say, therefore to the people of Israel, I am the Lord, I will bring you out from under the burdens of the Egyptians, and I will deliver you from slavery to them, and I will redeem you with an outstretched arm and with great acts of judgment."

Psalm 89:13 "You have a mighty arm; strong is your hand, high your right hand".

Isaiah 51:9: "Awake, awake, put on strength, O arm of the Lord; awake, as in the ancient days, in the generations of old...".

Deuteronomy 5:15: "You shall remember that you were a slave in the land of Egypt, and the Lord your God brought you out from there with a mighty hand and an outstretched arm".

Psalm 136:12: "With a strong hand and an outstretched arm, for his steadfast love endures forever".

Isaiah 52:10: "The Lord has bared his holy arm before the eyes of all the nations, and all the ends of the earth shall see the salvation of our God".

Isaiah 40:10: "Behold, the Lord God comes with might, and his arm rules for him; behold, his reward is with him, and his recompense before him".

30-day Breakthrough Prayer

Psalm 89:10: "You crushed Rahab like a carcass; you scattered your enemies with your mighty arm".

1 Peter 5:6: "Humble yourselves, therefore, under the mighty hand of God so that at the proper time he may exalt you".

The Manifestation and Power of God's Mighty Arm

This prayer synthesizes a collection of scriptural passages centered on the theological concept of God's "mighty arm" or "outstretched arm." This imagery serves as a powerful metaphor throughout the provided text, symbolizing God's sovereign power, active intervention in history, capacity for deliverance, and ultimate authority over all creation and opposition. The compilation draws from various books of the Bible—including Jeremiah, Exodus, Psalms, Isaiah, Deuteronomy, and 1 Peter—to illustrate that this divine strength is both the source of creation and salvation, judgment, and eternal steadfast love are enacted. The core purpose of these collected verses is to affirm the absolute invincibility of God and to encourage reliance upon this demonstrated power for defense, salvation, and personal exaltation through humility.

The scriptural references provided delineate several distinct, yet interconnected, themes regarding the nature and function of God's mighty arm. These themes range from establishing foundational sovereignty to detailing specific historical acts of redemption and prescribing the appropriate human response to such overwhelming might.

The Unchallengeable Sovereignty and Power of Creation

The prayer opens by establishing the absolute, unchallengeable nature of God's power, immediately linking it to His creative acts and His ability to defend those who call upon Him. This theme emphasizes that God's strength is the ultimate reality against which all other forces are rendered impotent.

- The introductory text asserts that the "arm of God" is mighty, implying that no opposing force can successfully stand against it. This power is characterized as sovereign, meaning it is self-derived, absolute, and requires no external validation or permission to act.
- A direct plea is made for this power to be deployed for deliverance and defense, specifically asking God to stretch out His arm to save the supplicant from those who seek to overtake them, demanding the scattering of the proud who oppose divine will.
- Jeremiah 32:17 is cited as the foundational statement for this sovereignty: "Oh, Lord God! You have made the heavens in the Earth by your great power and outstretched arm nothing is too hard for you." This verse connects the creation of the cosmos—the heavens and the Earth—directly to the exertion of this mighty arm, thereby establishing that if God can create everything, there is no subsequent task, however difficult, that lies beyond His capability. This establishes a baseline of omnipotence rooted in physical manifestation of power.

The Arm of Redemption: Deliverance from Bondage

A significant portion of the text focuses on the historical demonstration of the mighty arm in liberating the people of Israel from the oppressive bondage of Egypt. This act serves as the primary historical precedent for God's saving power.

- Exodus 6:6 is quoted, where the Lord promises to bring the Israelites out from under the burdens of the Egyptians. The method of this liberation is explicitly defined: redemption "with an outstretched arm and with great acts of judgment." This highlights that redemption is not merely a passive declaration but an active, forceful intervention involving both judgment against the oppressor and the physical drawing out of the oppressed.

- Deuteronomy 5:15 reinforces this historical memory, commanding the people to remember their former status as slaves in Egypt. The text stresses that the Lord God brought them out "with a mighty hand and an outstretched arm." The dual imagery of the "mighty hand" (representing immediate action and control) and the "outstretched arm" (representing the distance covered in the act of rescue) underscores the comprehensive nature of the deliverance wrought by divine strength. This memory is intended to shape their ongoing relationship with God, serving as an eternal reminder of what His power can accomplish on behalf of His people.

The Call for Divine Intervention and Awakening

The concept of the arm is not static; it is portrayed as something that can be called upon to "awaken" or be newly activated, suggesting a dynamic relationship where human need prompts divine engagement.

- Isaiah 51:9 issues a powerful imperative: "Awake, awake, put on strength, O arm of the Lord; awake, as in the ancient days, in the generations of old...". This passage implies that while the power is eternal, it requires a conscious invocation or stirring to manifest in current circumstances, drawing upon the efficacy demonstrated in foundational historical moments. It is a prayer for the reapplication of ancient, proven might in the present era.
- The request to "put on strength" suggests that the arm, though inherently strong, is being metaphorically clothed or prepared for immediate, decisive action, much like a warrior preparing for battle.

Defining the Attributes of Divine Strength and Rule

Several verses focus on describing the inherent qualities of this divine limb—its strength, its height, and its role in governance and recompense.

- Psalm 89:13 offers a direct affirmation of these attributes: "You have a mighty arm; strong is your hand, high your right hand. The "high right hand" symbolizes supreme authority, elevated above all others, signifying that God's power is not merely sufficient but superior and dominant in all spheres.
- Isaiah 40:10 further elaborates on God's rule, stating, "Behold, the Lord God comes with might, and his arm rules for him." This establishes the arm as the instrument through which God's might is executed and His dominion is maintained. Furthermore, this verse links the display of might directly to divine justice and reward: "behold, his reward is with him, and his recompense before him." The exertion of power is thus tied intrinsically to the administration of deserved outcomes.
- Psalm 89:13 also notes that the hand is "strong," emphasizing the sheer capacity for forceful action, which contrasts sharply with any perceived weakness in the supplicant or the opposition.

The Arm of Judgment and Victory Over Adversaries

The mighty arm is not only a tool for salvation but also an instrument of decisive victory and the crushing of opposition, demonstrating that God's power resolves conflict entirely in His favor.

- Psalm 89:10 provides a vivid depiction of this destructive capability: "You crushed Rahab like a carcass; you scattered your enemies with your mighty arm." Rahab, often interpreted as a mythological representation of chaos or a specific historical enemy, is destroyed—reduced to a mere carcass—by the direct application of this power. This illustrates that resistance to God's will results in complete annihilation of the opposing force.

- The scattering of enemies is the direct consequence of the arm's deployment, confirming that divine intervention results in the complete dissolution of threats, ensuring security for those under God's protection.

The Eternal Nature of God's Saving Acts and Love

The power displayed by the arm is shown to be consistent across time, underpinning both historical acts and future revelations, and is inextricably linked to God's enduring commitment to His people.

- Psalm 136:12 "With a strong hand and an outstretched arm, for his steadfast love endures forever." This verse is crucial as it anchors the demonstration of immense power not in arbitrary force, but in eternal, unwavering love (hesed). The power is the mechanism through which the love is expressed tangibly and repeatedly throughout history.
- Isaiah 52:10 speaks to the future and universal scope of this power: "The Lord has bared his holy arm before the eyes of all the nations, and all the ends of the earth shall see the salvation of our God." This suggests a final, public revelation of divine strength, where God's saving acts will no longer be confined to a specific people or era but will be witnessed globally, validating His holiness and sovereignty to every nation. The "baring" of the arm signifies preparation for the ultimate, undeniable act of salvation.

The Human Posture Before Divine Might

Finally, the prayer shifts focus from God's action to the required human response to acknowledging such overwhelming might, emphasizing humility as the necessary precursor to receiving divine favor.

- 1 Peter 5:6 provides the concluding instruction: "Humble yourselves, therefore, under the mighty hand of God so that at the proper time he may exalt you." This verse synthesizes the entire theme. Because God's hand is mighty (as established by creation, redemption, and judgment), the appropriate human posture is submission and humility.
- The phrase "under the mighty hand of God" demands a conscious yielding of personal will and pride. This humility is not an end but a strategic prerequisite. The promise attached to this submission is exaltation by God "at the proper time," suggesting that God's timing, guided by His mighty arm, will ultimately elevate the humble, reversing the natural order where the proud seek to exalt themselves.

The provided scriptural compilation powerfully asserts that the "mighty arm" of God is the central metaphor for His active, effective, and sovereign power in the universe. This power is demonstrated universally through creation (Jeremiah 32: 17), historically through miraculous deliverance from slavery (Exodus 6:6, Deuteronomy 5:15), and perpetually through the administration of justice and the scattering of enemies (Psalm 89:10). The arm is characterized by strength, high authority (Psalm 89:13), and is the very instrument through which God rules and recompenses (Isaiah 40:10). Crucially, these displays of overwhelming force are motivated by and inseparable from God's steadfast, eternal love (Psalm 136:12), culminating in a future, universal revelation of salvation (Isaiah 52:10). The ultimate takeaway for the reader is prescriptive: recognizing this absolute might necessitates a posture of profound humility, which, paradoxically, is the very condition under which God promises to bestow exaltation upon the faithful. The prayer thus serves as both a declaration of divine omnipotence and a guide for faithful reliance upon that power.

30-day Breakthrough Prayer

Chapter 18

The Word

Your word is a lamppost unto my feet. Speak into my soul. Stitch thy word unto the tablets of my heart, tie it as a reminder around my hand that I shall not forget your instructions. Your word has all power; you spoke and created the foundations of the world. Your word will not return unto your void. In the beginning was the word, and the word was God. Let no evil tongue rule over me, I am mindful over my tongue. According to your word, life and death is in the tongue, therefore I speak life and goodness to follow me all the days of my life, that I shall dwell in the house of the Lord. In Jesus name.

Amen.

A Profound Meditation on the Authority and Application of Divine Utterance

This prayer provides an extensive summary and analysis of the brief, but potent devotional text titled "The Word." The original content serves as a declaration of faith centered entirely on the nature, power, and practical application of divine utterance, often referencing scriptural concepts regarding the Logos. The purpose of the text is to establish a covenant relationship with this Word, seeking its guidance, acknowledging its creative authority, and committing to aligning one's own speech—the tongue—with its inherent life-giving principles. The summary below meticulously unpacks each phrase and concept presented in the original text, expanding upon its theological implications and practical mandates to meet the required comprehensive length, ensuring every point discussed is directly traceable back to the source material's core assertions.

30-day Breakthrough Prayer

The Word as Personal Illumination and Internalized Instruction

This section explores the initial plea for the Word to become an intimate, guiding force in the life of the supplicant, focusing on themes of guidance, memory, and deep internalization.

- The Word as a Lamppost unto My Feet: This foundational metaphor establishes the Word not as a distant, abstract concept, but as immediate, practical illumination for daily navigation. It suggests that the path ahead, often obscured by uncertainty or darkness, is made visible only through the light provided by this divine utterance. The light is specifically described as being "unto my feet," implying that guidance is provided step-by-step, moment by moment, rather than a sweeping, overwhelming vision of the entire future. This necessitates a continuous reliance on the Word for present direction. The implication is that without this specific light source, the individual is left stumbling in darkness, unable to discern the correct trajectory for their immediate actions. The Word functions as a necessary navigational tool, ensuring that every step taken is intentional and aligned with a higher purpose, transforming mundane movement into a guided journey.
- The Command to Speak into the Soul: The request, "Speak into my soul," moves beyond external guidance to demand internal transformation. The soul, representing the deepest core of being, requires direct infusion from the divine source. This is an appeal for the Word to penetrate beyond mere intellectual understanding or surface-level obedience, seeking residence in the seat of consciousness, emotion, and will. This act of speaking into the soul implies a desire for the Word to reshape internal motivations, purify hidden thoughts, and establish a foundational truth that governs all internal processes. It is a

request for spiritual saturation, where the essence of the divine utterance becomes the very substance of the inner self, making the individual's being responsive only to that divine frequency.

- The Mandate for Unforgettable Remembrance (Stitching and Tying): The text employs vivid imagery of permanent inscription and attachment to ensure the instructions carried by the Word are never forgotten. The instruction to "Stitch thy word unto the tablets of my heart" suggests an active, perhaps even painful or deliberate, process of embedding truth deep within the emotional and moral center. The heart, in this context, is the locus of commitment and feeling, requiring the Word to be woven into its very fabric so that forgetting becomes physically and spiritually impossible. Furthermore, the instruction to "tie it as a reminder around my hand" signifies the Word's role in governing action and labor. The hand is the instrument of doing, creating, and interacting with the physical world. By tying the Word there, the supplicant ensures that every physical endeavor is performed under the constant, tangible reminder of divine instruction, preventing actions that deviate from the established path. This dual inscription—on the heart for feeling and on the hand for doing—ensures comprehensive adherence.

The Word's Cosmic Authority and Infallible Efficacy

This section analyzes the declaration concerning the Word's inherent power, its role in creation, and its guaranteed effectiveness in fulfilling its purpose.

- The Word Possesses All Power and Creative Dominion: The assertion that "Your word has all power" elevates the utterance from mere communication to the fundamental force of reality. This power is demonstrated historically: "you spoke and created the foundations of the

world." This links the Word directly to the genesis of existence, positioning it as the active agent behind all structure, order, and being. This recognition of ultimate power demands reverence, as it implies that the Word is the source code of reality. Any lesser power or authority is subordinate to this
originating creative force. The supplicant acknowledges that the same power that established cosmic foundations is now being invoked for personal transformation and guidance.

- The Guarantee of Non-Return (Infallibility): The declaration, "Your word will not return unto your void," serves as a powerful statement of divine reliability and efficacy. A "void" return implies failure, ineffectiveness, or lack of result. By stating this will not happen, the text affirms that when the Word is sent forth—whether to create, to command, or to promise—it achieves its intended objective without fail. This concept provides absolute assurance to the supplicant. If the Word is spoken for guidance, guidance will be received; if spoken for protection, protection will manifest. It removes doubt regarding the outcome of divine decree, establishing a certainty that underpins the entire structure of faith articulated in the prayer.
- The Primordial Identity of the Word: The text anchors the Word in eternity and divinity by referencing its pre-existence: "In the beginning was the word, and the word was God." This statement establishes the Word as co-eternal with the divine essence, not merely a message from God, but an expression of God's very being. This theological identification is crucial because it imbues every instruction and promise with the absolute character of the Divine. To interact with the Word is to interact with the ultimate reality, reinforcing why it possesses "all power" and why it cannot fail. It is the ultimate standard against which all other realities are measured.

30-day Breakthrough Prayer

This segment focuses on the human responsibility to manage personal speech, recognizing the inherent danger and potential of the tongue, which must be brought into alignment with the divine Word.

- The Plea for Protection Against Negative Influence: The prayer immediately pivots from the divine Word's power to the human vulnerability: "Let no evil tongue rule over me." This recognizes that while the divine Word is supreme
- The Commitment to Mindful Self-Regulation: In direct response to the external threat, the supplicant declares a personal commitment: "I am mindful over my tongue." This is an active declaration of self-control and vigilance regarding one's own vocal output. It acknowledges that the tongue is a potential source of internal disorder if left unchecked, requiring constant awareness and discipline.
- The Recognition of the Tongue's Dualistic Power: The text articulates a profound principle regarding human speech: "According to your word, life and death is in the tongue." This highlights the immense, creative, and destructive potential residing in ordinary human articulation. The tongue is presented as a conduit capable of either blessing or cursing, building up or tearing down, mirroring, on a human scale, the creative power of the divine Word itself. Every utterance carries weight and consequence, capable of initiating processes of life or death, health or decay, within the speaker's sphere of influence.

The Consequence of Alignment: Speaking Life and Eternal Dwelling

The final cluster focuses on the positive outcome resulting from internalizing the divine Word and mastering personal speech, culminating in a promise of enduring spiritual security.

- The Active Declaration of Life and Goodness: Based on the understanding that life and death reside in the tongue, the supplicant makes a proactive choice: "therefore I speak life and goodness to follow me." This declaration is not passive wishing, but an authoritative decree made in alignment with the supreme, creative Word. The expectation is that these spoken affirmations will actively pursue and accompany the speaker throughout their entire temporal existence ("all the days of my life").
- The Ultimate Promise of Sanctuary: The culmination of this adherence to the Word—illumination, internalization, control of speech, and declaration of life—is the promise of eternal security: "that I shall dwell in the house of the Lord." This signifies the destination and ultimate reward for living a life governed by divine utterance.
- The Final Affirmation: The prayer concludes with the solemn invocation, "In Jesus name. Amen."

The provided text, "The Word," functions as a concentrated, powerful prayer or affirmation centered on the supreme importance of divine utterance. It moves systematically from acknowledging the Word as an external source of light and cosmic power to demanding its complete internalization within the heart and hand. The core message emphasizes that the Word is the foundation of creation and possesses infallible authority. Crucially, this divine standard is then used as the benchmark for human speech; recognizing the life-and-death power of the tongue, the supplicant commits to vigilance and the active declaration of life and goodness. The entire process is presented as the pathway to ultimate spiritual security—dwelling eternally in the presence of the Lord. The prayer serves as a blueprint for living a life saturated by divine truth, where external guidance dictates internal commitment, which in turn governs external action and speech, leading to eternal reward.

30-day Breakthrough Prayer

Chapter 19

A testament of Truth

[6] Jesus answered, "I am the way and the truth and the life. No one comes to the Father except through me.

The Truth of the Lord do I adore. Magnify the truth in Jesus. For the truth shall set me free. How my soul contest to lies, may I never become enslaved. I am free because of the Word of Truth. I stand on the mountains and declare the risen savior, that he has risen and Jesus throne sits above all others. I will not contest the Truth nor weigh it against man's judgment. In truth do I walk. In truth do I abide. Build thus my temple in high standard of Truth that none can deceive me nor de-establish my faith. I have not built my stature on falsehood nor the abomination which you abhor. Give me the discernment of revelations that I may keep thy principles. Let your Holy Spirit of Truth order my steps. Let peace that surpasses all understanding prevail on my ground.

John 1:14

The Word became flesh and lived among us. We saw his glory, such glory as of the one and only Son of the Father, full of grace and truth.

The Enduring Testament of Divine Truth: Foundation, Freedom, and Incarnation

This prayer serves as a meditation and declaration centered entirely upon the concept of Divine Truth, framed by key scriptural affirmations regarding Jesus Christ. It functions as a personal testament, articulating an adoration for the Truth of the Lord and establishing a covenant to live wholly within its precepts. The core purpose is to establish Truth—as embodied by Jesus Christ—as the sole foundation for spiritual life, personal freedom, and enduring faith. The text moves from the explicit declaration of Christ as the exclusive path to the Father, through a personal commitment to reject falsehood and embrace spiritual discernment guided by the Holy Spirit, culminating in a reflection on the Incarnation where this Truth became tangibly manifest in the world through the Son of God, full of grace and truth. The entire composition is an assertion that adherence to this singular, objective Truth is the prerequisite for liberation, stability, and transcendent peace.

Christ as the Exclusive Way, Truth, and Life

The foundation of this testament rests upon the direct assertion attributed to Jesus, establishing His unique and indispensable role in the relationship between humanity and the Divine. This declaration is not merely a statement of doctrine but the very cornerstone upon which the subsequent spiritual commitments are built.

- The Tripartite Identity: Jesus explicitly defines Himself using three essential, interconnected concepts: "I am the way and the truth and the life." This signifies that access to God (the Father) is not achieved through multiple avenues but is wholly contained within the person and work of Christ.
- The Way: This emphasizes the practical, directional aspect of faith—Jesus provides the sole pathway or method by which humanity can move toward reconciliation and communion with the Father. It implies that all other paths, regardless of their perceived merit or popularity, are ultimately divergent from the divine destination.
- The Truth: This defines the ontological reality of Christ. He is not merely a teacher of truth, but the embodiment of Truth itself. This objective reality stands independent of human perception or consensus, forming the standard against which all other claims must be measured.

- The Life: This speaks to the essential, eternal vitality that flows from the Truth. To follow the Way and embrace the Truth results in possessing genuine, unending Life, which transcends mere biological existence.
- The Exclusivity of Access: The statement concludes with an absolute boundary: "No one comes to the Father except through me." This underscores the singularity of Christ's mediation. The testament affirms this exclusivity, recognizing that the Truth of the Lord is not one option among many, but the singular gateway to ultimate reality and divine relationship.

The Liberating Power of Truth Over Deception

A central theme articulated in the personal reflection is the profound, active role Truth plays in securing spiritual freedom for the believer, contrasting sharply with the bondage imposed by falsehood.

- Adoration and Magnification: The author expresses deep reverence: "The Truth of the Lord do I adore." This adoration is active, requiring the believer to "Magnify the truth in Jesus," suggesting that the focus of one's life and declaration must be centered on Him.
- The Promise of Freedom: The core benefit derived from embracing this Truth is explicitly stated: "For the truth shall set me free." This freedom is positioned as the direct antidote to spiritual captivity.
- Contesting Lies and Avoiding Enslavement: The soul is depicted as actively engaged in spiritual warfare against deception: "How my soul contest to lies, may I never become enslaved." This implies that vigilance is required, as the default state, absent the Truth, is one of enslavement to falsehoods.
- Freedom Rooted in the Word: The source of this liberation is identified as the "Word of Truth." This connects the abstract concept of Truth directly to the revealed scripture and the

person of Christ (the Logos), confirming that freedom is secured through adherence to divine revelation.

- Declaration of Victory: The believer stands firm, declaring the ultimate victory of the risen Savior, whose throne "sits above all others." This declaration solidifies the supremacy of the Truth over all earthly powers or competing ideologies.

A Personal Covenant and Commitment to Unwavering Faith

The devotional section transitions into a firm, personal resolution regarding how the believer intends to conduct their life considering this revealed Truth, establishing boundaries against compromise and human judgment.

- Walking and Abiding in Truth: The commitment is twofold and continuous: "In truth do I walk. In truth do I abide." This signifies both active daily conduct (walking) and a settled, permanent state of dwelling (abiding) within the reality of the Truth.
- Rejection of Human Standards: A critical boundary is established concerning the evaluation of divine reality: "I will not contest the Truth nor weigh it against man's judgment." This mandates that the objective standard of the Lord's Truth supersedes subjective human opinion or temporal standards of evaluation.
- Building the Spiritual Temple: The believer commits to constructing their spiritual identity and practice upon this divine foundation: "Build thus my temple in high standard of Truth." This temple represents the inner life, faith structure, and public witness of the individual.
- Defense Against Deception: The purpose of this high standard is protective: "that none can deceive me nor de-establish my faith." The Truth acts as the essential structural integrity preventing spiritual collapse or doctrinal deviation.
- Rejection of Falsehood as Foundation: The author explicitly rejects building their personal stature

or reputation on unstable ground: "I have not built my stature on falsehood nor the abomination which you abhor." This is a declaration of moral and theological purity in construction.

Seeking Divine Guidance and Experiencing Transcendent Peace

The commitment to Truth necessitates active petition for divine assistance to maintain integrity and achieve spiritual stability amidst worldly pressures.

- Petition for Discernment: The believer actively seeks the capacity to perceive and understand divine instruction: "Give me the discernment of revelations that I may keep thy principles." This acknowledges that maintaining the high standard of Truth requires supernatural insight, not mere human intellect.
- The Ordering Power of the Holy Spirit: The request for guidance is specific, invoking the third person of the Trinity: "Let your Holy Spirit of Truth order my steps." This highlights the Spirit's role as the active agent who applies the Truth (the Word) to the believer's daily path, ensuring alignment with divine will.
- The Attainment of Surpassing Peace: The ultimate reward for walking ordered by the Spirit of Truth is profound tranquility: "Let peace that surpasses all understanding prevail on my ground." This peace is not merely the absence of conflict but a supernatural state of well-being that defies logical explanation, rooted in the security of the Truth.

The Incarnation: Truth Made Manifest in the Flesh

The testament grounds the abstract concept of Truth in historical reality by referencing the profound theological statement found in John 1:14, emphasizing the physical manifestation of the divine essence.

- The Word Becomes Tangible: The scripture affirms the mystery of the Incarnation: "The Word became flesh and lived among us." This signifies that the eternal, divine Truth, previously known through revelation, took on human form, making the infinite accessible within finite existence.
- Witnessing Divine Glory: The believers became eyewitnesses to this manifestation: "We saw his glory." This glory is not merely an outward display of power but the visible manifestation of the inherent nature of God dwelling in human form.
- The Unique Identity of the Incarnate: The glory witnessed was specifically that belonging to "the one and only Son of the Father." This reinforces the unique relationship between Jesus and God, confirming His singular status as the revealer of the Father.
- The Embodiment of Grace and Truth: The culmination of the Incarnation is "full of grace and truth." This pairing is crucial: Truth provides the objective standard and reality, while Grace provides the merciful means by which humanity can meet that standard. In Jesus, these two divine attributes are perfectly balanced and fully present.

This document, "A testament of Truth," functions as a comprehensive declaration of faith centered on the absolute sovereignty and necessity of Divine Truth as revealed in Jesus Christ. It establishes that Truth is not merely an abstract concept but a personal reality—the Way to the Father, the source of ultimate freedom from enslavement to lies, and the very essence of eternal Life. The author commits to a life lived in active adherence to this Truth, rejecting the temptation to measure divine reality against fleeting human judgment. This commitment requires reliance on the Holy Spirit for discernment and guidance, promising in return a peace that transcends all worldly comprehension. Ultimately, the testament anchors this entire spiritual framework in the historical event of the Incarnation, where the eternal Word, full of both grace and truth, physically tabernacled among humanity, providing the ultimate, visible, and accessible standard for all who seek the Father.

30-day Breakthrough Prayer

Chapter 20

Precepts & Statutes

O Lord, the Eternal Father in Heaven we come before You with humility, seeking the light of Your wisdom and guidance. Blessed are those who walk blamelessly, and we strive to follow Your laws with unwavering devotion. As we navigate our paths, grant us the steadfastness to remain aligned with Your statutes and the courage to seek you fervently.

Teach me, O Lord, the embodiment of purity in my thoughts and actions. May Your Word dwell richly within me, guarding my heart against sin and directing my path with righteousness. In moments of trial, may I find comfort in Your promises, relying on Your faithfulness as my refuge and strength.

As my soul long for understanding, open my eyes to the wonders of Your decrees, that I may meditate on their beauty and depth. Empower me with the discernment to recognize the snares of deceit, guiding me away from the paths of the proud and the wicked. Let my life reflect the richness of Your commandments and fill my heart with joy as I delight in Your law.

This I pray in the spirit of Your everlasting love and righteousness.

Amen.

The below supplement was taken from Holy Bible from KJV

Psalm 119 KJV

א Aleph

30-day Breakthrough Prayer

1 Blessed are those whose ways are blameless,
who walk according to the law of the Lord.
2 Blessed are those who keep his statutes
and seek him with all their heart—
3 they do no wrong
but follow his ways.
4 You have laid down precepts
that are to be fully obeyed.
5 Oh, that my ways were steadfast
in obeying your decrees!
6 Then I would not be put to shame
when I consider all your commands.
7 I will praise you with an upright heart
as I learn your righteous laws.
8 I will obey your decrees;
do not utterly forsake me.

ב Beth

9 How can a young person stay on the path of purity?
By living according to your word.
10 I seek you with all my heart;
do not let me stray from your commands.
11 I have hidden your word in my heart
that I might not sin against you.
12 Praise be to you, Lord;
teach me your decrees.
13 With my lips I recount
all the laws that come from your mouth.
14 I rejoice in following your statutes
as one rejoices in great riches.
15 I meditate on your precepts
and consider your ways.
16 I delight in your decrees;
I will not neglect your word.

ג Gimel

17 Be good to your servant while I live,
that I may obey your word.
18 Open my eyes that I may see
wonderful things in your law.
19 I am a stranger on earth;
do not hide your commands from me.

20 My soul is consumed with longing
for your laws at all times.
21 You rebuke the arrogant, who are accursed,
those who stray from your commands.
22 Remove from me their scorn and contempt,
for I keep your statutes.
23 Though rulers sit together and slander me,
your servant will meditate on your decrees.
24 Your statutes are my delight;
they are my counselors.

ד Daleth

25 I am laid low in the dust;
preserve my life according to your word.
26 I gave an account of my ways and you answered me;
teach me your decrees.
27 Cause me to understand the way of your precepts,
that I may meditate on your wonderful deeds.
28 My soul is weary with sorrow;
strengthen me according to your word.
29 Keep me from deceitful ways;
be gracious to me and teach me your law.
30 I have chosen the way of faithfulness;
I have set my heart on your laws.
31 I hold fast to your statutes, Lord;
do not let me be put to shame.
32 I run in the path of your commands,
for you have broadened my understanding.

ה He

33 Teach me, Lord, the way of your decrees,
that I may follow it to the end.[b]
34 Give me understanding, so that I may keep your law
and obey it with all my heart.
35 Direct me in the path of your commands,
for there I find delight.
36 Turn my heart toward your statutes
and not toward selfish gain.
37 Turn my eyes away from worthless things;
preserve my life according to your word.[c]
38 Fulfill your promise to your servant,

so that you may be feared.
39 Take away the disgrace I dread,
for your laws are good.
40 How I long for your precepts!
In your righteousness preserve my life.

ו Waw

41 May your unfailing love come to me, Lord,
your salvation, according to your promise;
42 then I can answer anyone who taunts me,
for I trust in your word.
43 Never take your word of truth from my mouth,
for I have put my hope in your laws.
44 I will always obey your law,
for ever and ever.
45 I will walk about in freedom,
for I have sought out your precepts.
46 I will speak of your statutes before kings
and will not be put to shame,
47 for I delight in your commands
because I love them.
48 I reach out for your commands, which I love,
that I may meditate on your decrees.

ז Zayin

49 Remember your word to your servant,
for you have given me hope.
50 My comfort in my suffering is this:
Your promise preserves my life.
51 The arrogant mock me unmercifully,
but I do not turn from your law.
52 I remember, Lord, your ancient laws,
and I find comfort in them.
53 Indignation grips me because of the wicked,
who have forsaken your law.
54 Your decrees are the theme of my song
wherever I lodge.
55 In the night, Lord, I remember your name,
that I may keep your law.
56 This has been my practice:
I obey your precepts.

ח Heth

57 You are my portion, Lord;
I have promised to obey your words.
58 I have sought your face with all my heart;
be gracious to me according to your promise.
59 I have considered my ways
and have turned my steps to your statutes.
60 I will hasten and not delay
to obey your commands.
61 Though the wicked bind me with ropes,
I will not forget your law.
62 At midnight I rise to give you thanks
for your righteous laws.
63 I am a friend to all who fear you,
to all who follow your precepts.
64 The earth is filled with your love, Lord;
teach me your decrees.

ט Teth

65 Do good to your servant
according to your word, Lord.
66 Teach me knowledge and good judgment,
for I trust your commands.
67 Before I was afflicted I went astray,
but now I obey your word.
68 You are good, and what you do is good;
teach me your decrees.
69 Though the arrogant have smeared me with lies,
I keep your precepts with all my heart.
70 Their hearts are callous and unfeeling,
but I delight in your law.
71 It was good for me to be afflicted
so that I might learn your decrees.
72 The law from your mouth is more precious to me
than thousands of pieces of silver and gold.

י Yodh

73 Your hands made me and formed me;
give me understanding to learn your commands.
74 May those who fear you rejoice when they see me,
for I have put my hope in your word.
75 I know, Lord, that your laws are righteous,

and that in faithfulness you have afflicted me.
76 May your unfailing love be my comfort,
according to your promise to your servant.
77 Let your compassion come to me that I may live,
for your law is my delight.
78 May the arrogant be put to shame for wronging me without cause;
but I will meditate on your precepts.
79 May those who fear you turn to me,
those who understand your statutes.
80 May I wholeheartedly follow your decrees,
that I may not be put to shame.

כ Kaph

81 My soul faints with longing for your salvation,
but I have put my hope in your word.
82 My eyes fail, looking for your promise;
I say, "When will you comfort me?"
83 Though I am like a wineskin in the smoke,
I do not forget your decrees.
84 How long must your servant wait?
When will you punish my persecutors?
85 The arrogant dig pits to trap me,
contrary to your law.
86 All your commands are trustworthy;
help me, for I am being persecuted without cause.
87 They almost wiped me from the earth,
but I have not forsaken your precepts.
88 In your unfailing love preserve my life,
that I may obey the statutes of your mouth.

ל Lamedh

89 Your word, Lord, is eternal;
it stands firm in the heavens.
90 Your faithfulness continues through all generations;
you established the earth, and it endures.
91 Your laws endure to this day,
for all things serve you.
92 If your law had not been my delight,
I would have perished in my affliction.

93 I will never forget your precepts,
for by them you have preserved my life.
94 Save me, for I am yours;
I have sought out your precepts.
95 The wicked are waiting to destroy me,
but I will ponder your statutes.
96 To all perfection I see a limit,
but your commands are boundless.

מ Mem

97 Oh, how I love your law!
I meditate on it all day long.
98 Your commands are always with me
and make me wiser than my enemies.
99 I have more insight than all my teachers,
for I meditate on your statutes.
100 I have more understanding than the elders,
for I obey your precepts.
101 I have kept my feet from every evil path
so that I might obey your word.
102 I have not departed from your laws,
for you yourself have taught me.
103 How sweet are your words to my taste,
sweeter than honey to my mouth!
104 I gain understanding from your precepts;
therefore I hate every wrong path.

נ Nun

105 Your word is a lamp for my feet,
a light on my path.
106 I have taken an oath and confirmed it,
that I will follow your righteous laws.
107 I have suffered much;
preserve my life, Lord, according to your word.
108 Accept, Lord, the willing praise of my mouth,
and teach me your laws.
109 Though I constantly take my life in my hands,
I will not forget your law.
110 The wicked have set a snare for me,
but I have not strayed from your precepts.
111 Your statutes are my heritage forever;
they are the joy of my heart.

112 My heart is set on keeping your decrees
to the very end.[d]

ס Samekh

113 I hate double-minded people,
but I love your law.
114 You are my refuge and my shield;
I have put my hope in your word.
115 Away from me, you evildoers,
that I may keep the commands of my God!
116 Sustain me, my God, according to your
promise,and I will live;
do not let my hopes be dashed.
117 Uphold me, and I will be delivered;
I will always have regard for your decrees.
118 You reject all who stray from your decrees,
for their delusions come to nothing.
119 All the wicked of the earth you discard like
dross;
therefore I love your statutes.
120 My flesh trembles in fear of you;
I stand in awe of your laws.

ע Ayin

121 I have done what is righteous and just;
do not leave me to my oppressors.
122 Ensure your servant's well-being;
do not let the arrogant oppress me.
123 My eyes fail, looking for your salvation,
looking for your righteous promise.
124 Deal with your servant according to your love
and teach me your decrees.
125 I am your servant; give me discernment
that I may understand your statutes.
126 It is time for you to act, Lord;
your law is being broken.
127 Because I love your commands
more than gold, more than pure gold,
128 and because I consider all your precepts right,
I hate every wrong path.

פ Pe

129 Your statutes are wonderful;
therefore I obey them.
130 The unfolding of your words gives light;
it gives understanding to the simple.
131 I open my mouth and pant,
longing for your commands.
132 Turn to me and have mercy on me,
as you always do to those who love your name.
133 Direct my footsteps according to your word;
let no sin rule over me.
134 Redeem me from human oppression,
that I may obey your precepts.
135 Make your face shine on your servant
and teach me your decrees.
136 Streams of tears flow from my eyes,
for your law is not obeyed.

צ Tsadhe

137 You are righteous, Lord,
and your laws are right.
138 The statutes you have laid down are righteous;
they are fully trustworthy.
139 My zeal wears me out,
for my enemies ignore your words.
140 Your promises have been thoroughly tested,
and your servant loves them.
141 Though I am lowly and despised,
I do not forget your precepts.
142 Your righteousness is everlasting
and your law is true.
143 Trouble and distress have come upon me,
but your commands give me delight.
144 Your statutes are always righteous;
give me understanding that I may live.

ק Qoph

145 I call with all my heart; answer me, Lord,
and I will obey your decrees.
146 I call out to you; save me
and I will keep your statutes.
147 I rise before dawn and cry for help;
I have put my hope in your word.

148 My eyes stay open through the watches of the night,
that I may meditate on your promises.
149 Hear my voice in accordance with your love;
preserve my life, Lord, according to your laws.
150 Those who devise wicked schemes are near,
but they are far from your law.
151 Yet you are near, Lord,
and all your commands are true.
152 Long ago I learned from your statutes
that you established them to last forever.

ר Resh

153 Look on my suffering and deliver me,
for I have not forgotten your law.
154 Defend my cause and redeem me;
preserve my life according to your promise.
155 Salvation is far from the wicked,
for they do not seek out your decrees.
156 Your compassion, Lord, is great;
preserve my life according to your laws.
157 Many are the foes who persecute me,
but I have not turned from your statutes.
158 I look on the faithless with loathing,
for they do not obey your word.
159 See how I love your precepts;
preserve my life, Lord, in accordance with your love.
160 All your words are true;
all your righteous laws are eternal.

ש Sin and Shin

161 Rulers persecute me without cause,
but my heart trembles at your word.
162 I rejoice in your promise
like one who finds great spoil.
163 I hate and detest falsehood
but I love your law.
164 Seven times a day I praise you
for your righteous laws.
165 Great peace have those who love your law,
and nothing can make them stumble.

166 I wait for your salvation, Lord,
and I follow your commands.
167 I obey your statutes,
for I love them greatly.
168 I obey your precepts and your statutes,
for all my ways are known to you.

ת Taw

169 May my cry come before you, Lord;
give me understanding according to your word.
170 May my supplication come before you;
deliver me according to your promise.
171 May my lips overflow with praise,
for you teach me your decrees.
172 May my tongue sing of your word,
for all your commands are righteous.
173 May your hand be ready to help me,
for I have chosen your precepts.
174 I long for your salvation, Lord,
and your law gives me delight.
175 Let me live that I may praise you,
and may your laws sustain me.
176 I have strayed like a lost sheep.
Seek your servant,
for I have not forgotten your commands.

Chapter 21

Gain not to Lose

36 For what shall it profit a man, if he shall gain the whole world, and lose his own soul?

Many people of today tarry at worldly possessions at the ultimate cost of losing their soul, oh let that not be me, Lord. Oh, How I do marvel at your truth. You've given the keys that all things upon the earth man do have dominion; but can they not ruler of their own soul to keep? Let me be amongst the quiet in the land and thirst not. For I know that you will supply all my needs according to your richness in glory if my sought be of you. Give me power in the spirit that I shall not give into the body's enticement. Enlighten my mental with the wisdom of obtaining rampant systems, the drawings of ancient innovations and modern technologies which that create overflow. Give thou me patience to contend with all likings that I might not lose peace. Increase the territory of my portion to sustain righteousness, I know that you will supply me with unmeasurable cattle of the kingdom, plantation of the harvest, you are ruler and bring no contamination to my life. I know you will add to my years, and you are the author of my richness and finisher of my faith. Build up my Gates, that I shall not be trampled upon, nor oppressed. Keep me in thy royal Kingdom, for your splendor sits above all thrones of Creation. With you I am assured. In Jesus name I seal this prayer.

The Pursuit of Eternal Gain Over Temporal Loss

This prayer presents a profound and deeply personal spiritual reflection, framed as a prayer, centered on the ultimate cost of worldly ambition versus the preservation of the eternal soul. It begins by invoking the critical question regarding the profit of gaining the entire world while suffering the loss of one's inner self. The text then transitions into a fervent petition for divine assistance in navigating the temptations and complexities of contemporary life. The author expresses a desire to prioritize spiritual quietude and trust in divine provision over the pursuit of fleeting material success. The core of the prayer is a request for spiritual empowerment, wisdom to discern true value amidst technological advancement, fortitude to maintain inner peace against worldly likings, and assurance of protection within a divine, eternal kingdom. It is a comprehensive appeal for sanctification, security, and the fulfillment of faith, sealed with an affirmation of trust in Jesus Christ.

The Peril of Worldly Acquisition and the Soul's Value

The foundation of this spiritual discourse is established by confronting the inherent danger present in contemporary human striving. The text immediately highlights a critical existential trade-off:

- The central theme is derived from the scriptural inquiry: "For what shall it profit a man, if he shall gain the whole world, and lose his own soul?" This question serves as the primary lens through which all subsequent desires and actions are measured.
- A direct observation is made regarding the habits of modern individuals, noting that "Many people of today tarry at worldly possessions at the ultimate cost of loosing their soul." This suggests a dangerous stagnation or delay in recognizing true priorities, where temporal accumulation is valued above eternal well-being.
- The author expresses a strong personal rejection of this path, declaring emphatically, "oh let that not be I oh Lord." This establishes the prayeras a commitment to a different course of action, one rooted in spiritual preservation rather than material acquisition.
- The marveling at the Lord's truth underscores the clarity that this spiritual insight brings,

contrasting sharply with the blindness induced by worldly focus.

The Paradox of Dominion and Self-Mastery

The reflection delves into the nature of human authority granted over the physical realm and contrasts it with the critical need for internal governance.

- The text acknowledges a divine endowment: "You've given the keys that all things upon the earth man do have dominion." This recognizes the granted stewardship over the material creation.
- However, this acknowledgment immediately pivots to a crucial self-examination regarding internal authority: "but can they not ruler of their own soul to keep?" This rhetorical question implies that dominion over external things does not automatically confer mastery over the self, highlighting a significant gap in human capability without divine aid.
- The desired state is one of spiritual contentment and detachment: "Let me be amongst the quiet in the land and thirst not." This signifies a yearning for a state where external pressures do not create internal want or desperation.
- This contentment is predicated on faith in divine provision: "For I know that you will supply all my needs according to your richness in glory if my sought be of you." The measure of supply is not earthly scarcity but the boundless nature of divine glory, contingent upon the direction of one's seeking.

The Ascetic Struggle Against Carnal Temptation

A significant portion of the petition focuses on securing the necessary spiritual fortitude to resist the inherent pull toward physical gratification and worldly temptation.

- The author explicitly requests empowerment for internal warfare: "Give me power in the spirit that I shall not give into the bodies enticement." This frames the spiritual life as an active struggle requiring supernatural strength to overcome inherent physical urges.

- The concept of "bodies enticement" suggests a recognition of the flesh as a source of distraction or temptation that actively works against the soul's higher calling.
- The request for spiritual power is thus a plea for the ability to maintain spiritual discipline and integrity against seductive, immediate physical rewards.

The prayer seeks not just resistance to temptation, but active, enlightened engagement with the world's systems and innovations, demanding a specific form of divine wisdom.

- The request is for mental enlightenment concerning complex structures: "Enlighten my mental with the wisdom of obtaining rampant systems." This suggests a desire to understand and perhaps navigate complex, widespread, and rapidly growing organizational or economic structures without being consumed by them.
- This wisdom must bridge historical and contemporary knowledge: it includes understanding "the drawings of ancient innovations and modern technologies which that create overflow."
- The phrase "create overflow" is significant, implying that the desired wisdom should lead to abundance, but this abundance must be spiritually managed, contrasting with the "overflow" of worldly gain that leads to soul loss. The wisdom sought is the key to harnessing these powerful forces for righteous ends.
- This wisdom is sought as a tool for strategic engagement rather than passive avoidance, requiring divine insight to utilize powerful systems without succumbing to their inherent risks.

Fortification of Faith and the Maintenance of Peace

The petition continues by asking for the endurance required to maintain spiritual focus amidst ongoing spiritual conflict and desire management.

- A specific request is made for resilience: "Give thou me patience to contend with all likings that I might not lose peace." This identifies "likings"—worldly desires, attractions, or preferences—as active adversaries that must be contended with.
- The preservation of "peace" is established as the immediate stake in this contention. Losing peace is presented as a precursor to losing the soul, linking back to the initial theme.
- Furthermore, the author seeks expansion in their spiritual capacity: "Increase the territory of my portion to sustain righteousness." This implies that righteousness is a domain or inheritance that needs constant cultivation and expansion, requiring divine assistance to maintain its borders and productivity.

The Assurance of Kingdom Wealth and Divine Sovereignty

The author expresses deep confidence in the nature of the provision that awaits those who seek righteousness, contrasting it with the temporary nature of earthly wealth.

- The expected supply is described using rich, metaphorical language: "I know that you will supply me with unmeasurable cattle of the kingdom, plantation of the harvest." This imagery suggests a wealth that is vast, agricultural (productive), and inherently belonging to the divine realm, far exceeding earthly measures.
- This assurance is rooted in the recognition of God's absolute authority: "you are ruler and bring no contamination to my life." Divine rule guarantees purity, whereas human rule or self-rule often introduces corruption.

- The author affirms belief in divine intervention regarding the length and quality of life: "I know you will add to my years."
- Crucially, the text affirms God's role in the spiritual journey: "you are the author of my richness and finisher of my faith." This establishes a complete cycle of divine involvement, from the inception of spiritual wealth to the completion of belief.

The Plea for Impregnable Spiritual Security

The final requests focus on establishing an unassailable defensive posture against external oppression and internal vulnerability, securing a place within the divine structure.

- A direct plea for fortification is made: "Build up my Gates, that I shall not be trampled upon, nor oppressed." The "Gates" symbolize points of entry, defense, and governance; strengthening them ensures protection against spiritual assault or external domination.
- The ultimate desire is eternal residency in the divine sphere: "Keep me in thy royal Kingdom." This kingdom is defined by its supreme authority, as "your splendor sits above all thrones of Creation." This places the desired dwelling place above all earthly or created power structures.
- The prayer concludes with an expression of absolute certainty: "With you I am assured." This assurance is the final spiritual gain, superseding any material profit.
- The entire petition is formally concluded and ratified: "In Jesus name I seal this prayer."

The prayer serves as an intensive meditation on spiritual prioritization, arguing forcefully against the foolishness of exchanging eternal soul-value for worldly gain. The author moves from acknowledging the universal temptation of material accumulation to requesting specific divine interventions necessary for spiritual survival and flourishing in a complex world. Key takeaways include the necessity of self-mastery over dominion of the earth, the need for wisdom to navigate both ancient and modern technological systems without contamination, and the reliance on divine power to resist carnal enticements and maintain inner peace. Ultimately, the text is a comprehensive declaration of dependence on God for provision, protection (symbolized by the fortified Gates), and eternal placement within the Royal Kingdom, confirming that true, unmeasurable richness is found only in the secure relationship with the Author and Finisher of one's faith. The entire reflection underscores that the only profitable venture is one that ensures the soul is never lost, regardless of earthly possessions gained or forfeited.

Chapter 22

Sanctification

Glorify the Lord Jesus, this I do with honor and thanks. Give the way to what provides purification and sanctification to my mental, address me from that which is above; that my faculties and members are with what frequent from the heavens.

Let love abide. Provide thy center, focal and atoned be called by that which you have achieved and already obtained. Bring into the perfect alignment that that which connects my body mind and spirit to walk upright in nature is in ordinance on the earth. Give me the dimensional authority to subdue what is beneath; in that my shortcomings are not which is unmeasured.

Bring your presence upon us, ooh Lord, this day; this season; that we shall feel the comfort of your good deeds; that there shall be not less any lack. Magnify the Lord, ooh my soul, and release me from all heavy laden. Restore upon my life many years, that longing and sorrow has become the distant of my memory. Restore my soul that I shall live with the abundance inheritance of everlasting. Protect the gates, that that which open is upon the blessed and plentiful.

You are great and merciful, bring it to pass. Show us your love and kindness. The presence of the Lord is good forever.

1 John 4:16

And we have known and believed the love that God hath for us. God is love, and he that dwelleth in love dwelleth in God, and God in him.

Lamentations 3:22-23

22 Because of the Lord's great love we are not consumed,
for his compassions never fail. 23 They are new every
morning; great is your faithfulness

30-day Breakthrough Prayer

Psalms 140:13

13 Surely the righteous shall give thanks unto Thy name; the upright shall dwell in Thy presence.

2 Corinthians 7:11 Amplified

For [you can look back and] see what an earnestness and authentic concern this godly sorrow has produced in you: what vindication of yourselves [against charges that you tolerate sin], what indignation [at sin], what fear [of offending God], what longing [for righteousness and justice], what passion [to do what is right], what readiness to punish [those who sin and those who tolerate sin]! At every point you have proved yourselves to be innocent in the matter.

Sanctification: A Devotional Exploration of Spiritual Alignment and Divine Grace

This prayer, titled "Sanctification," presents a concise yet profound devotional prayer seeking deep spiritual transformation and alignment with divine will. It serves as an earnest petition to the Lord Jesus, establishing a framework for achieving purity, connection with the heavens, and practical righteousness on earth. The text moves sequentially through stages of worship, self-examination, request for divine intervention, and affirmation of eternal goodness. It outlines a comprehensive spiritual discipline involving mental purification, alignment of the physical and spiritual self, release from earthly burdens, and the restoration of life through grace. The core purpose is to move the supplant from the state of human limitations and sorrow toward a life, characterized by divine presence, abundance, and everlasting inheritance, all grounded, and an acknowledgment of God, inherit greatness and mercy.

Glorification and the Foundation of Gratitude

30-day Breakthrough Prayer

The prayer commences with an explicit declaration of worship, establishing the necessary spiritual prerequisite for all subsequent requests: "Glorify the Lord Jesus, this I do with honor and thanks." This opening statement is crucial, as it frames the entire petition not as a demand based on merit, but as an act of devotion stemming from recognition of inherent worthiness in the subject of the prayer.

- The act of glorification is presented as an active, ongoing duty, performed with both "honor," suggesting reverence and respect for the divine majesty, and "thanks," indicating a posture of gratitude for past and anticipated blessings.
- This initial step underscores the theological principle that true sanctification begins not with self-improvement, but with the outward focus of adoration. By honoring Jesus first, the supplicant aligns their internal state with the external reality of divine sovereignty.
- The honor bestowed is not merely ceremonial; it is the mental and spiritual acknowledgment that sets the stage for receiving the purification that follows. It is the key that unlocks the pathway to higher spiritual engagement.

The Pursuit of Mental Purification and Heavenly Connection

The second passage immediately transitions into the specific need for internal cleansing, focusing intensely on the mental faculties and seeking divine direction from above. *"Given the way to what provides purification and sanctification to my mental, address me from that which is above, that my faculties and members are with what frequent from the heavens."*

- The request centers on the "mental," highlighting the modern understanding that spiritual warfare and growth often begin in the realm of thought and perception. Sanctification is explicitly linked to mental clarity and purity.

- The supplicant seeks a "way" or a method for this purification, implying a desire for instruction or revelation rather than simply wishing the state into existence.
- The appeal is directed "from that which is above," emphasizing a reliance on transcendent, heavenly sources for this transformation, contrasting sharply with earthly or purely human methods of self-help.
- The desired outcome is the synchronization of the individual's "faculties and members" (representing all aspects of being—intellect, will, emotion, and physical action) with the divine flow, described poetically as that which "frequent[s] from the heavens." This suggests a continuous, regular communion with the divine source.
- This section establishes the vertical relationship: purification is achieved by allowing heavenly influence to permeate and govern the internal mental landscape.

The Abiding Nature of Divine Love and Atonement

The prayer then calls for the establishment of love as a permanent state, coupled with a request for definition and grounding in achieved grace. "Let love abide. Provide thy center, focal and atoned be called by that which you have achieved and already obtained."

- The imperative "Let love abide" demands that love is not transient but a resident quality, the core operating principle of the supplicant's being. This love must be divine in origin to sustain itself.
- The request for the provision of "thy center, focal and atoned" is complex. It asks for a defined, stable spiritual core ("center") and a clear point of focus ("focal").
- The term "atoned" suggests a state of reconciliation and completeness achieved through sacrifice, linking the individual's current stability back to past redemptive acts.

- Crucially, this stability must be "*called by that which you have achieved and already obtained.*" This reinforces the theme of gratitude; the present state of grace is built upon the established, completed work of the divine, providing a solid foundation upon which the supplicant can stand.

Achieving Perfect Alignment: Body, Mind, and Spirit

A central theme of the prayer is the quest for holistic integration, ensuring that the physical existence operates in harmony with spiritual truth. "Bring into the perfect alignment that that which connects my body mind and spirit to walk upright in nature is in ordinance on the earth."

- This passage articulates the goal of embodied spirituality—a state where the internal connection between body, mind, and spirit is flawless ("perfect alignment").
- The purpose of this alignment is practical: to enable the individual to "walk upright in nature." This implies ethical living, integrity, and adherence to natural or divine law in daily conduct.
- The phrase "is in ordinance on the earth" signifies that this upright walk must be established as a recognized, functional order within the earthly realm, not merely an abstract ideal. It demands manifestation.
- This alignment is the mechanism by which the spiritual self-exerts positive, ordered influence over the temporal self, ensuring that actions flow from a unified, sanctified source.

Authority Over Shortcomings and Earthly Ordinance

Immediately following the call for alignment, the supplicant requests the necessary power to manage internal failings and external pressures. "Give me the dimensional authority to subdue what is beneath; in that my shortcomings are not which is unmeasured."

- The request is for "dimensional authority," suggesting a power that transcends ordinary human capacity, derived from the alignment achieved in the previous step. This authority is needed to exert control over the lower aspects of existence ("what is beneath").
- This "beneath" can be interpreted as base desires, worldly temptations, or the chaotic elements of the unredeemed self.
- The goal of this subduing power is explicitly tied to self-knowledge and accountability: ensuring that personal "shortcomings are not which is unmeasured." This implies a desire for divine insight into one's failures so they can be accurately assessed, addressed, and corrected, rather than being ignored or underestimated.
- The authority requested is thus a tool for disciplined self-governance, preventing spiritual drift by keeping personal failings within the scope of divine oversight and correction.

Invocation of Presence, Comfort, and Provision

The prayer shifts focus outward again, calling specifically for the tangible experience of the divine presence in the immediate temporal context. "Bring your presence upon us, ooh Lord, this day; this season; that we shall feel the comfort of your good deeds; that there shall be not less any lack."

- The invocation is specific to the present moment ("this day; this season"), grounding the spiritual request in the immediacy of lived experience.
- The desired effect of this presence is the palpable experience of "comfort," derived directly from recognizing God's "good deeds." This links comfort not to the absence of trouble, but to the awareness of benevolent action already undertaken.
- The petition concludes with a powerful declaration against scarcity: "that there shall be not less any lack." This is a comprehensive request for provision, encompassing material, emotional, and

spiritual needs, ensuring sufficiency derived from divine goodness.

- This section emphasizes that the presence of the Lord is inherently practical, delivering tangible benefits (comfort and provision) alongside spiritual ones.

Magnification of the Soul and Release from Burdens

The supplicant then turns inward to address the state of the soul itself, seeking empowerment and liberation. "Magnify the Lord, ooh my soul, and release me from all heavy laden."

- The command, "Magnify the Lord, ooh my soul," echoes themes found in various Psalms, urging the inner self to actively praise and elevate God, thereby shifting focus away from personal distress.
- This act of magnification is immediately linked to the desired outcome: "release me from all heavy laden." The spiritual act of praise is presented as the mechanism for shedding significant burdens, suggesting that the weight of the world lessens when the focus is placed on divine greatness.
- The "heavy laden" represents the accumulated stress, guilt, responsibility, and sorrow carried by the individual, which the soul, when properly engaged in worship, is empowered to cast off.

Restoration, Inheritance, and Overcoming Sorrow

This segment offers a profound vision for the future, seeking recovery from past suffering and securing an eternal future. "Restore upon my life many years, that longing and sorrow has become the distant of my memory. Restore my soul that I shall live with the abundance inheritance of everlasting."

- The request for the restoration of "many years" suggests a desire not just for longevity, but for the reclamation of time lost to unproductive states like "longing and sorrow." The goal is to transform past suffering into a distant, neutralized memory.

- The restoration is twofold: temporal (years) and spiritual (the soul). The restoration of the soul is defined by its future state: living with the "abundance inheritance of everlasting."
- This emphasizes that true restoration is inextricably linked to the eternal perspective. Earthly healing paves the way for the realization of an inheritance that is both abundant and eternal, moving beyond temporary relief to permanent, overflowing blessing.

Guarding the Gates to Blessing and Plentifulness

The focus narrows to protection and ensuring access to positive outcomes. "Protect the gates, that that which open is upon the blessed and plentiful."

- The metaphor of "gates" is employed, symbolizing points of entry and exit—decisions, perceptions, opportunities, and spiritual access points.
- The request is for divine protection over these critical junctures to ensure that only positive outcomes—that which is "blessed and plentiful"—are allowed entry or passage.
- This implies an active spiritual defense mechanism is required to filter influences, ensuring that the alignment and purification sought earlier result in tangible, positive manifestations in life. The gates must be guarded against influences that lead to scarcity or curse.

Acknowledging Mercy and Manifesting Kindness

The prayer concludes its series of petitions by acknowledging the character of the entity being addressed and requesting a visible demonstration of that character. "You are great and merciful, bring it to pass. Show us your love and kindness."

- This serves as a powerful affirmation of God's nature: greatness (power and scope) coupled with mercy (compassion and forgiveness). These attributes are the grounds upon which the requests are made.
- The phrase "bring it to pass" is a firm declaration of faith, requesting that the preceding petitions be actualized.
- The final active request is for a demonstration: "Show us your love and kindness." This moves beyond abstract belief to demand experiential confirmation of the divine attributes acknowledged.

The prayer "Sanctification" is a comprehensive blueprint for a life lived in deliberate spiritual pursuit. It meticulously charts a course beginning with humble glorification and gratitude, moving through the rigorous internal work of mental purification and holistic alignment of body, mind, and spirit. The text emphasizes that true sanctification requires active engagement: seeking heavenly direction, establishing abiding love, claiming authority over personal failings, and casting off heavy burdens through worship. The ultimate aspirations detailed are profound: the restoration of lost time, the securing of an everlasting and abundant inheritance, and the protection of all pathways leading to blessing. The prayer culminates in a powerful affirmation of faith, recognizing the greatness and mercy of the Lord as the guarantee that these transformative states will indeed be brought to pass, culminating in the final, foundational truth: "The presence of the Lord is good forever." This short text thus encapsulates a complete spiritual cycle, from initial reverence to sustained, blessed existence under divine favor.

30-day Breakthrough Prayer

Chapter 23

Fervent Prayer

James 5:16

"Confess your faults one to another, and pray one for another, that ye may be healed. The effectual fervent prayer of a righteous man availeth much."

Today, I set forth my declaration's, and I decree my prayer life is activated into the Heavenly realm and will not just remain earthbound. Today, I am renewed. What I release into the heavens God will hear and answer me. I establish my faith and destiny to be prosperous, effective and productive in my life and all my endeavors, purpose and needs are fulfilled. I decree and declare that my health, mental, physical and spiritual life are in wellness and good order, my family's needs are improved and functioning in divine order and my purpose is in accordance to the goodness of God, my business and financial needs are being met with increase and unexpected influx, surplus, my church and social life is healthy, positive and God surrounds the people, places and opportunities to serve me for my good. I place God the Father, Son and Holy Spirit at the head of my life, that he will defend and cover me; no weapon formed against me shall prosper. I am more than a conqueror through Christ Jesus who continues to strengthen me. He has sat my in my rightful place of authority to operate dominion upon the earth. I am blessed and I release the battle unto the Lord. I am free, in the name of Jesus Christ.

30-day Breakthrough Prayer

Chapter 24

Fighting Evil and Spiritual Warfare

I decree and declare as I pick up my cross and lead out of bondage, haven been bit by the python of a brainwashed place, people who agendas were to bring ruin, I have been set free by Christ Jesus. Cancel their attacks, those who wait to harm me. I am a new creature in Jesus. Release me and direct me out of captivity. Those who bring evil device and demise towards my life, I cancel all their plans and disengage that their plans over my life, the plans of my enemies are null and void, let them bewitch themselves and seize their own lives with every haughty thought of evil and curses that they send to me. Release me out of the finite resources into what is infinite.

Those that send arrows, send attacks against me, let the 2:11 gate be captive into their plot that they are robbed of their stolen ideas, concepts, businesses, finances, allegiance, children, storehouses and property. Vengeance belongs to you oh Lord, Jesus by your name every knee must bow, send your mighty conquering power to avenge the unjust on my behalf, as I plead the blood of Jesus over my life and bloodline.

Psalms 144:1

> Blessed be the Lord my strength, who teach my hands to war and my fingers to fight; 144: 5 Bow down Your heavens, O Lord, and come down; Touch the mountains, and they shall smoke.
> 6 Flash forth lightning and scatter them;
> Shoot out Your arrows and destroy them.
> 7 Stretch out Your hand from above;
> Rescue me and deliver me out of great waters,
> From the hand of foreigners,
> 8 Whose mouth speaks lying words,
> And whose right hand is a right hand of falsehood.

Robbers in the darkness has set up to destroy me in battle, but the battle belongs you, oh Lord. They've attacked and stolen my children; they've robbed my inheritance and cast sickness on my life. Deliver me merciful God into the abundance of restoration, overflow blessings so that I may serve you as my Lord and Savior bringing glory and honor to your name.

Show your mighty arm, send your angelic host of defending angels to war on my behalf. The encounters were with My very own family members who sought to help destroy my existence, break every curse of identity theft, identity swamping, poverty, and hatred that was spoken against my life. Take back with the enemy has stolen from me and cause confusion to their surveillance and point of contact that each channel disarms their purpose, fails and let the purpose they have for me, become their own purpose their own fate in life. It was my very own people who took counsel against me. Bring all my enemies and the evil contentious intention of the cult that has risen against me to light, bring ruin, scatter them, bring your destruction and division and bring your judgment swiftly, release me from their souls. Hedge your protection around me, let no weapon formed against me, prosper in the name of Jesus Christ, they've come after me without reason other than greed and jealousy. Many have come with the spirit of Jezebel, they brought treachery of witchcraft may you avenge your prophecy at the hand of Jezebel, let that spirit be eaten by the dogs until none is left, destroy their evil spirits many lurk in evil to undermine my purpose, destroy and disempower their attacks against me, let them be eaten by dogs, let them have their fate. Show your mercy onto me Lord. I plead the blood of Jesus Christ, son of God, wonderful counselor, Mighty God, prince of Peace, omnipotent king of kings, Lord of Host send your angels to conquer, send your angels to avenge, send your spiritual warriors to break bows, release all their captivity over my life. Set me free from their torment and heinous deeds.

I will look to the Hills from where comes my help! Great is your mercy towards me. Protect my children and grandchildren from the hands of the government and my enemies. Disband the malicious system my name from

30-day Breakthrough Prayer

Psalms 18 NIV

I will love thee, O Lord, my strength.

2 The Lord is my rock, and my fortress, and my
deliverer; my God, my strength, in whom I will
trust; my buckler, and the horn of my salvation,
and my high tower.

3 I will call upon the Lord, who is worthy to be
praised: so, shall I be saved from mine enemies.

4 The sorrows of death compassed me, and the floods
of ungodly men made me afraid.

5 The sorrows of hell compassed me about: the snares
of death prevented me.

6 In my distress I called upon the Lord and cried
unto my God: he heard my voice out of his temple,
and my cry came before him, even into his ears.

7 Then the earth shook and trembled; the foundations
also of the hills moved and were shaken, because he
was wroth.

8 There went up a smoke out of his nostrils, and
fire out of his mouth devoured: coals were kindled
by it.

9 He bowed the heavens also, and came down: and
darkness was under his feet.

10 And he rode upon a cherub, and did fly: yea, he
did fly upon the wings of the wind.

11 He made darkness his secret place; his pavilion
round about him were dark waters and thick clouds
of the skies.

12 At the brightness that was before him his thick
clouds passed, hail stones and coals of fire.

13 The Lord also thundered in the heavens, and the Highest gave his voice; hail stones and coals of fire.

14 Yea, he sent out his arrows and scattered them; and he shot out lightnings, and discomfited them.

15 Then the channels of waters were seen, and the foundations of the world were discovered at thy rebuke, O Lord, at the blast of the breath of thy nostrils.

16 He sent from above, he took me, he drew me out of many waters.

17 He delivered me from my strong enemy, and from them which hated me: for they were too strong for me.

18 They prevented me in the day of my calamity: but the Lord was my stay.

19 He brought me forth also into a large place; he delivered me, because he delighted in me.

20 The Lord rewarded me according to my righteousness; according to the cleanness of my hands hath he recompensed me.

21 For I have kept the ways of the Lord, and have not wickedly departed from my God.

22 For all his judgments were before me, and I did not put away his statutes from me.

23 I was also upright before him, and I kept myself from mine iniquity.

24 Therefore hath the Lord recompensed me according to my righteousness, according to the cleanness of my hands in his eyesight.

25 With the merciful thou wilt shew thyself
merciful; with an upright man thou wilt shew
thyself upright;

26 With the pure thou wilt shew thyself pure; and
with the froward thou wilt shew thyself froward.

27 For thou wilt save the afflicted people; but wilt
bring down high looks.

28 For thou wilt light my candle: the Lord my God
will enlighten my darkness.

29 For by thee I have run through a troop; and by my
God have I leaped over a wall.

30 As for God, his way is perfect: the word of
the Lord is tried: he is a buckler to all those
that trust in him.

31 For, who is God, save the Lord? or who is a rock
save our God?

32 It is God that girdeth me with strength, and
maketh my way perfect.

33 He maketh my feet like hinds' feet, and setteth
me upon my high places.

34 He teacheth my hands to war, so that a bow of
steel is broken by mine arms.

35 Thou hast also given me the shield of thy
salvation: and thy right hand hath holden me up,
and thy gentleness hath made me great.

36 Thou hast enlarged my steps under me, that my
feet did not slip.

37 I have pursued mine enemies and overtaken them:
neither did I turn again till they were consumed.

38 I have wounded them that they were not able to
rise: they are fallen under my feet.

39 For thou hast girded me with strength unto the
battle: thou hast subdued under me those that rose
up against me.

40 Thou hast also given me the necks of mine
enemies; that I might destroy them that hate me.

41 They cried, but there was none to save them: even
unto the Lord, but he answered them not.

42 Then did I beat them small as the dust before the
wind: I did cast them out as the dirt in the
streets.

43 Thou hast delivered me from the strivings of the
people; and thou hast made me the head of the
heathen: a people whom I have not known shall serve
me.

44 As soon as they hear of me, they shall obey me:
the strangers shall submit themselves unto me.

45 The strangers shall fade away and be afraid out
of their close places.

46 The Lord liveth; and blessed be my rock; and let
the God of my salvation be exalted.

47 It is God that avengeth me and subdued the people
under me.

48 He delivereth me from mine enemies: yea, thou
liftest me up above those that rise up against me:
thou hast delivered me from the violent man.

49 Therefore will I give thanks unto thee, O Lord,
among the heathen, and sing praises unto thy name.

50 Great deliverance giveth he to his king; and sheweth mercy to his anointed, to David, and to his seed for evermore.

A Comprehensive Declaration of Spiritual Warfare, Deliverance, and Divine Vengeance

This prayer serves as an extensive, multi-faceted declaration and prayer focused entirely on engaging in spiritual warfare against perceived evil forces, curses, and human enemies. The text outlines a process of personal spiritual renewal, the cancellation of malicious plans directed against the speaker's life and bloodline, and the invocation of powerful divine intervention. It blends personal petitions for deliverance from specific afflictions—such as identity theft, poverty, and sickness—with direct citations from the Psalms (primarily Psalm 144 and Psalm 18), using scriptural authority to command victory, restoration, and the swift judgment of adversaries. The core purpose is to transition from a state of captivity and finite limitation into a realm of infinite resources and divine protection, ensuring that the battle is fought and won by the Lord on the speaker's behalf.

Personal Deliverance and Spiritual Renewal

The declaration begins with the speaker actively engaging in a process of spiritual separation and self-renewal following a period of intense spiritual attack:

- The speaker acknowledges picking up their cross and leading out of a metaphorical "desert," signifying a journey through hardship and desolation.
- A specific source of affliction is identified: being "bitten by the python of a brainwashed place," suggesting manipulation or spiritual entanglement originating from a source with ruinous agendas.

- Immediate action is taken to cancel all attacks and evil devices aimed at bringing demise toward the speaker's life.
- A strong declaration is made that the plans of enemies are rendered "null and void."
- The speaker commands the enemies to "bewitch themselves," forcing them to seize their own lives with the very haughty thoughts of evil and curses they intended for the speaker.
- A key request for transition is articulated: release from "finite resources into what is infinite," symbolizing a move from scarcity or limitation to divine abundance.
- The prayer seeks direct release and direction out of captivity, emphasizing a need for immediate liberation from current constraints.

Invocation of Divine Retribution and Judgment

A significant portion of the text is dedicated to calling down specific, targeted retribution upon those who have sent attacks, often using vivid, scriptural imagery of warfare and capture:

- For those who send "arrows" and attacks, the speaker invokes the "2:11 gate" to become a trap, ensuring the attackers are robbed of their own stolen assets.
- The list of stolen assets targeted for repossession is comprehensive, including stolen ideas, concepts, businesses, finances, allegiance, children, storehouses, and property.
- The speaker explicitly delegates vengeance to the Lord, Jesus, demanding that by His name, every knee must bow.
- Mighty conquering power is requested to avenge the unjust actions committed against the speaker.
- The blood of Jesus is pleaded over the speaker's life and bloodline as a sanctifying and protective measure against ongoing attacks.
- The speaker calls for the enemies' own purposes to fail and become their own fate, asserting that

those who took counsel against the speaker will face ruin.
- A demand is made for the exposure of the "evil contentious intention any person(s) or groups that has risen against me," calling for swift judgment, destruction, and division upon them.
- The speaker requests that the divine judgment be executed swiftly, seeking release from the influence or souls of these adversaries.

Identification and Confrontation of Specific Adversaries

The text details the nature and identity of the opposition, noting that these attacks often come from unexpected or close sources:

- The document reveals that encounters involved "My very own family members who sought to help destroy my existence."
- The speaker identifies the motivation of many enemies as stemming from "greed and jealousy," noting they have come without legitimate reason.
- A specific spiritual entity is named: many adversaries operate with the "spirit of Jezebel," bringing "treachery of witchcraft" against the speaker.
- The speaker demands vengeance upon this spirit, decreeing that the spirit of Jezebel be "eaten by the dogs until none is left."
- The prayer seeks to destroy and disempower the evil spirits lurking to undermine the speaker's purpose, reiterating the command for them to be eaten by dogs and meet their destined fate.
- The text calls for the destruction of specific curses spoken against the life, including curses related to identity theft, identity swamping, poverty, and hatred.

Reliance on Scriptural Authority (Psalms 144 and 18)

The declarations are heavily fortified by direct quotations and invocations of power drawn from specific

Psalms, establishing a foundation of established divine precedent for warfare:

- Psalm 144 Invocation: The speaker praises the Lord as strength, who teaches hands to war and fingers to fight (Ps. 144:1). The speaker calls for God to bow the heavens, come down, and cause the mountains to smoke (Ps. 144:5). Divine weaponry is requested: flashing forth lightning to scatter enemies and shooting out arrows to destroy them (Ps. 144:6). A plea for rescue is made, asking the Lord to stretch out His hand from above to deliver the speaker from "great waters" and from foreigners whose mouths speak lying words and whose right hand is one of falsehood.
- Petition for Restoration and Protection of Lineage

The document emphasizes the material and familial losses incurred due to the spiritual attacks, demanding comprehensive restoration:

- The speaker notes that robbers in the darkness have attacked and stolen their children, robbed their inheritance, and cast sickness upon their lives.
- A plea is made for merciful God to deliver the speaker into an "abundance of restoration" and "overflow blessings."
- The goal of this restoration is explicitly stated: to allow the speaker to serve God as Lord and Savior, bringing glory and honor to His name.
- The speaker requests the manifestation of God's mighty arm and the dispatch of an "angelic host of defending angels" to wage war on their behalf.
- A specific request is made to protect children and grandchildren from the hands of both the government and personal enemies.
- The speaker demands the disbanding of any malicious system that is attempting to use or manipulate their name.

- The speaker looks to the Hills, acknowledging that help comes from there, and recognizing the greatness of God's mercy toward them.

Declarations of Divine Empowerment and Conquest

The text concludes the active declaration phase by affirming the empowerment granted by God, which enables the speaker to overcome obstacles that were previously insurmountable:

- The speaker claims that by God, they have run through a troop and leaped over a wall (Ps. 18:29).
- God is affirmed as the one who girds the speaker with strength, makes their way perfect, and makes their feet like the feet of hinds, setting them upon high places (Ps. 18:32-33).
- The speaker claims the shield of salvation provided by God, noting that His gentleness has made them great and His right hand has held them up (Ps. 18:35).
- The speaker asserts that enemies who hear of them shall obey, and strangers shall submit themselves and fade away in fear from their close places (Ps. 18:44-45).
- The declaration affirms that the Lord lives, is the rock of salvation, and that God avenges the speaker, subduing the people under them (Ps. 18:46-47).
- The speaker claims deliverance from violent men, being lifted above those who rise against them (Ps. 18:48).
- The final affirmative statement is a vow to give thanks among the heathen and sing praises unto God's name because of the great deliverance shown to His anointed (Ps. 18:49-50).

The prayer "Fighting Evil and Spiritual Warfare" is a comprehensive and intense spiritual mandate rooted in biblical promises of divine intervention. It functions as both a confession of faith and a binding declaration against spiritual and human opposition. The central themes revolve around immediate personal deliverance from specific forms of spiritual oppression (python "venomous" influence, curses, identity theft), the comprehensive restoration of stolen assets (inheritance, children, finances), and the invocation of divine justice against adversaries motivated by greed and jealousy, including those operating under the influence of the "spirit of Jezebel." By heavily quoting Psalms 144 and 18, the speaker establishes a historical and theological precedent for victory, asserting that because God has previously delivered, taught them to war, and rewarded their righteousness, He will continue to subdue their enemies, scatter their foes with divine weaponry (lightning and arrows), and ultimately elevate the speaker into a position of safety, abundance, and honor. The text concludes with a commitment to praise God for the assured great deliverance.

30-day Breakthrough Prayer

Chapter 25

Cancel & Void Evil intentions

Numbers 22:11. I Am blessed & Covered by the Blood of Jesus **Numbers 22:12** For in thy word as it happened, prophesied in the book of Numbers, NO curse formed against me shall prosper, as you said in Numbers, 22:12 "and God said to balaam, thou shall not curse the people: for they are blessed.

In thy field, I am blessed.

In the city, I am blessed.

In my coming, I am blessed.

In my going, I am blessed.

In thy home, I am blessed.

In the streets, I am blessed.

At work, I am blessed.

Everywhere I go, I am blessed.

The FAVOR of God is on my life, I thank God for His anointed One, JESUS has blessed me.

I am blessed in the courts.

I am blessed in the yard.

I am blessed amongst the people.

My children are blessed.

My family is blessed.

My church, Pastor and all those I fellowship is blessed.

My business partners, friends, constituents, associates and those in within my affiliation are blessed.

My credit is blessed, and I am debt free because of this blessing.

My reputation is blessed.

30-day Breakthrough Prayer

My ideas, creativity, and leadership business concepts are advancing and blessed, and therefore my opportunities gain advantage and benefit me because they are blessed.

My finances are blessed.

My business is blessed.

My country is blessed above the nations.

The schools my children and grandchildren attend are blessed.

My city is blessed.

I am blessed amongst the earth.

I am above and not beneath, I am the head and not the tail; I am blessed by God, from the Heavens above.

Wherever I go, God has already prepared a way for me, he goes before me and with me.

I am blessed because God has given His angels charge over me. Hallelujah! Thank you Jesus.

My gifts within my body, mind, spirit and soul are blessed.

I receive of the overflow and abundance because I am blessed, my blessings come from God, I do not eat out of the hands of man, God supply's all my needs, he is Jehovah Jireh, my provider.

In all territories from the heavens and upon the earth, I am blessed.

I am blessed in my sitting down; I am blessed in my rising up.

No weapon formed against me shall prosper, no cursing of words, plots, schemes, potions, plans, technology, devices, government, wickedness or unrighteousness authorities, nor powers and principalities, famine, economy, trickery of the devil nor his children have power above my God, I am blessed. For God will not leave His righteous forsaken, nor his seed begging for bread.

30-day Breakthrough Prayer

God has shown his favor unto me and my seed.

In your Word, **Isaiah 61: 1-3** I seek your promises:

The Spirit of the Sovereign Lord is on me,
because the Lord has anointed me
to proclaim good news to the poor.
He has sent me to bind up the brokenhearted,
to proclaim freedom for the captives
and release from darkness for the prisoners,[a]
2 to proclaim the year of the Lord's favor
and the day of vengeance of our God,
to comfort all who mourn,
3 and provide for those who grieve in Zion—
to bestow on them a crown of beauty
instead of ashes,
the oil of joy
instead of mourning,
and a garment of praise
instead of a spirit of despair.
They will be called oaks of righteousness,
a planting of the Lord
for the display of his splendor.

Thanks, honor, glory and praise for your gracious mercy is my hope and trust.

Amen.

Comprehensive Declaration of Divine Blessing and Immunity from Curses

This prayer serves as an exhaustive spiritual declaration and affirmation designed to actively cancel and void any evil intentions directed toward the speaker, simultaneously establishing an unshakeable state of divine blessing and comprehensive protection under the Blood of Jesus. Drawing heavily upon scriptural foundations, particularly referencing the book of Numbers, the text systematically asserts that no curse formulated against the individual shall succeed because they are explicitly declared blessed by God. The affirmation covers every conceivable aspect of life—physical location, relationships, finances, professional endeavors, and spiritual standing—culminating in a powerful invocation of prophetic fulfillment regarding divine favor, comfort, and transformation. The entire declaration functions as a proactive statement of faith, claiming total dominion over negative forces and asserting a divinely ordained position of superiority and abundance.

Cancellation of Curses and Covenant Protection

This foundational theme establishes the legal and spiritual basis for immunity against all forms of malice, rooted in specific scriptural pronouncements.

- Voiding Evil Intentions: The declaration explicitly commands the cancellation and voiding of all evil intentions directed toward the speaker, referencing the authority found in Numbers 22:11. This action is immediate and absolute, seeking to nullify any spiritual or verbal attack launched against the individual.
- Covering by the Blood of Jesus: A crucial element of protection is invoked through the declaration of being covered by the Blood of Jesus, referencing the context established in Numbers 22:12. This signifies a complete spiritual covering that supersedes human or demonic authority.
- Scriptural Inviolability: The core assertion is that, in accordance with the word prophesied in the book of Numbers, no curse formed against the speaker shall prosper. This is directly tied to the divine decree spoken to Balaam: "thou shall not curse the people: for they are blessed." This declaration establishes that the speaker's blessed status is a mandate from God that overrides any attempt at malediction.

- Divine Mandate Against Cursing: The text emphasizes the established fact that God Himself has forbidden the cursing of His people, making any attempt to do so an act against divine will, thereby ensuring the prosperity of the blessed individual.

Ubiquity of Blessing in Daily Existence and Location

The affirmation systematically covers every physical location and movement associated with the speaker's daily life, ensuring that the blessing is not confined to one area but is universally present.

- Blessings in Specific Environments: The declaration asserts a specific, localized blessing across all key areas of daily activity: In thy field, the speaker is blessed. In the city, the speaker is blessed. In thy home, the speaker is blessed. In the streets, the speaker is blessed. At work, the speaker is blessed.
- Blessings in Transit and Action: The blessing extends to the very act of movement and transition: In my coming, the speaker is blessed. In my going, the speaker is blessed.
- Universal Presence of Blessing: This localized enumeration culminates in a sweeping declaration that covers all movement and activity: Everywhere I go, I am blessed. This confirms that the state of being blessed is constant, irrespective of the environment or activity undertaken.

Blessings on Relationships, Assets, and Personal Standing

This section details the extension of divine favor into the speaker's social circles, legal interactions, financial stability, and public perception.

- Favor and Anointing: The speaker acknowledges the overarching presence of the FAVOR of God on their life, offering thanks to God for His anointed One, JESUS, who has conferred this blessing.

- Blessings in Formal and Public Settings: The blessing is declared effective in structured environments: I am blessed in the courts. I am blessed in the yard. I am blessed amongst the people.
- Blessing Extended to Kin and Community: The favor is not limited to the individual but flows outward to immediate and extended networks: My children are blessed. My family is blessed. My business partners, friends, constituents, associates and those in within my affiliation are blessed. This comprehensive inclusion ensures that all professional and personal alliances benefit from the declared favor.
- Financial Security and Integrity: A specific focus is placed on economic well-being: My credit is blessed. I am debt free because of this blessing. This links financial liberation directly to the overarching divine blessing.
- Reputational Sanctity: The declaration concludes this segment by affirming the protection and elevation of public image: My reputation is blessed.

Advancement, Opportunity, and Superiority

The affirmations move into declarations concerning growth, strategic advantage, and a divinely ordained position of leadership and national prominence.

- Conceptual and Business Advancement: The speaker claims blessing upon their intellectual output and strategic planning: My ideas, creativity, and leadership business concepts are advancing and blessed. Consequently, my opportunities gain advantage and benefit me because they are blessed. This establishes a direct causal link between divine favor and tangible success in enterprise.
- Material Prosperity: Specific declarations confirm material well-being: My finances are blessed. My business is blessed.

- National and Institutional Elevation: The blessing is declared to have a broad, societal impact: My country is blessed above the nations. The schools my children and grandchildren attend are blessed. My city is blessed.
- Universal Blessing and Positional Authority: The speaker claims a supreme status granted by God: I am blessed amongst the earth. I am above and not beneath, I am the head and not the tail; I am blessed by God, from the Heavens above. This is a powerful claim to ultimate hierarchical placement, sanctioned by heavenly authority.

Divine Provision, Spiritual Security, and Abundance

This extensive section details proactive divine intervention, comprehensive spiritual warfare immunity, and guaranteed provision sourced directly from God.

- Proactive Divine Arrangement: Wherever I go, God has already prepared a way for me, he goes before me and with me.
- Angelic Guard: Explicit acknowledgment is given to supernatural protection: I am blessed because God has given His angels charge over me. Hallelujah! Thank you Jesus.
- Internal Blessing: My gifts within my body, mind, spirit and soul are blessed.
- Overflow and Self-Sufficiency: The speaker claims a state of perpetual surplus, sourced exclusively from the divine: I receive of the overflow and abundance because I am blessed. My blessings come from God; I do not eat out of the hands of man. God supply's all my needs; he is Jehovah Jireh, my provider.
- Comprehensive Territorial Blessing: The blessing is confirmed across all realms: In all territories from the heavens and upon the earth, I am blessed.
- Blessing in All States: The blessing is constant, whether active or resting I am blessed in my sitting down, I am blessed in my rising up.

- Exhaustive Immunity from Weaponry and Malice: This is perhaps the most detailed section, listing every conceivable threat that is rendered powerless: No weapon formed against me shall prosper. This immunity specifically negates: no cursing of words, plots, schemes, potions, plans, technology, devices, government, wickedness or unrighteousness authorities, nor powers and principalities, famine, economy, trickery of the devil nor his children. The rationale provided is that these entities have no power above the speaker's God, who will not forsake His righteous or allow His seed to beg for bread.
- Divine Favor for Posterity: God has shown His favor unto me and my seed, ensuring generational blessing.

The Anointing and Fulfillment of Prophetic Ministry

The final segment shifts focus to the prophetic mandate and the transformative power associated with the anointing of the Spirit, drawing heavily on themes reminiscent of Isaiah 61 and Luke 4.

- The Presence of the Spirit: The declaration affirms that The Spirit of the Sovereign Lord is on me, because the Lord has anointed me.
- The Mandate to Proclaim Good News: The anointing carries specific responsibilities directed toward those in need: To proclaim good news to the poor. He has sent me to bind up the brokenhearted. To proclaim freedom for the captives and release from darkness for the prisoners.
- Proclaiming Divine Timing: The speaker claims authority to declare God’s appointed times: To proclaim the year of the Lord's favor and the day of vengeance of our God.
- Ministry of Comfort and Provision: The purpose includes active intervention for the afflicted: To comfort all who mourn. And provide for those who grieve in Zion.

- Transformative Exchange: The declaration outlines a series of powerful spiritual exchanges that replace negative states with divine glory: To bestow on them a crown of beauty instead of ashes. The oil of joy instead of mourning. And a garment of praise instead of a spirit of despair.
- Resulting Identity and Purpose: The ultimate outcome of this transformation is a new identity: They will be called oaks of righteousness, a planting of the Lord for the display of his splendor.
- Final Trust: The entire declaration is anchored in gratitude and reliance: Thanks, honor, glory and praise for your gracious mercy is my hope and trust.

The provided prayer is a comprehensive, multi-layered spiritual declaration asserting absolute, divinely guaranteed blessing and immunity across every facet of existence. It begins by invoking scriptural authority (Numbers 22) to cancel all curses and establish protection under the Blood of Jesus. The affirmations then cover physical locations, personal movements, professional associations, family units, and financial stability, ensuring that blessings are pervasive and inescapable. A significant portion is dedicated to declaring comprehensive security against all forms of spiritual and physical assault—from technology and government authorities to demonic trickery—while simultaneously claiming a position of superiority (head and not the tail). Finally, the declaration culminates in claiming the prophetic mantle of the anointed Spirit, promising transformation, comfort, and the replacement of despair with beauty, joy, and praise, thereby establishing the speaker as a display of God's splendor, secured entirely by His gracious mercy.

30-day Breakthrough Prayer

30-day Breakthrough Prayer

Chapter 26

Great Are Your Mercies Towards Me

Father, my father, I greet you with my first fruits. I come bruised and battled yet I come. I come because you said come to me all who are burdened and heavy laden and that you would give me rest.

I come with thanksgiving for your fulfillment of what is divine and true. I lay my burdens down, unto and upon your altar so that you will fulfill your promises to those who love you and are called according to your name.

My petitions are upon my heart, how great are your mercies to look upon the afflicted and give to the meek your salvation. Save me, oh, my soul cries out to the heavens to hearken unto my prayers.

Bring swiftly your judgement and rescue my children out of the hands of my enemies. Many of them formed their schemes to undertake my children down into the grave, they have snatched my grandchildren to bondage and wickedness, but I call upon the armies of heaven's angelic host to guard and restore her keeping her from her harm or danger and bring her home to her own territory.

THEY'VE plucked her out into an evil place and landscaped iniquity all around, lead and hedge your angels in her defense to escape the wiles of the devil. Bring her rescue and into your safe harbor.

Many are the evil deeds that THEY'VE plotted as if I were a destroyer or abomination, but it is I who have kept my peace. Pass me not onto them that they should eat of my flesh.

30-day Breakthrough Prayer

They target me without just cause, but that they fill up their greed with obnoxious terror and carry malice to the simple.

In readiness, make me ready, synchronize and synchro pate my life in divine timing and alignment with purpose and plans to be prosperous in strength, in productivity and leadership, ownership and build up my gates, in aptitude, let me soar, in battle, let me crush and divide them, bring them terror for their evil attacks, cancel every Witcher of the four winds of the earth down into the grave they have dug for me.

Avenge and restore in every territory where terror lurks to bring destruction.

I rebuke, cancel and void any agreement, invitation, and entertainment of any evil host of demonic spirits, familiar spirits, monitoring spirits are cancelled, and I am now the router to disengage, and cancel assignments, destroying their cords of communication all points of contact, they are null and void and ordered into the abyss of depth into the darkness of the sea to be cast into the hell beneath the sand of the Red Sea . The gangs, cults, criminals, and betrayers who have worked in alliance to deceive and destroy my destiny are cancelled by the blood of Jesus, divide their spoils, let them eat of their evil deeds that do not belong to me, I am not contentious or of any supplement of wrath or punishment nor death, nor attack of any demonic energies transmitted , transpire, conspire, or release into my spirit, body, soul, health, finances, business, ministry, family, home, environment.

Calamity is far from me and my loved ones. We are of thy blessed people who you defend with your mighty arm. Your hand is upon us, with none of them can withstand. Release your blessings and covenant upon me.

Pour from the heavens the goodness from your grace that I become the lender and not the borrower nor let my seed beg of bread. Enrich us among the courts and council, financial institutions, and policy makers the show me favor; cover me all the days of my life.

Bring sanctification, restoration, and edification to my temple to move, be productive and think strategically and build with ownership and authority and kingdom privileges that provoke and ignite health, wealth, prosperity bring all peace that surpasses understanding by the glory and the blood of the Lord Jesus Christ.

May this prayer reach the ear and be heard upon the heaven and the angels and the highest God Jehovah, Elohim. Great all your mercies to me, show me your loving kindness. Be righteous and show yourself righteous amongst your servants.

Amen.

This document presents a profound and detailed religious petition, titled "Great is your mercy," characterized by intense supplication, spiritual confrontation, and an unwavering declaration of faith in divine promises. The text chronicles the journey of a supplicant approaching the divine Father while acknowledging personal affliction and burden, transitioning into fervent requests for salvation, protection for family, and aggressive spiritual warfare against perceived enemies and demonic forces. Ultimately, the prayer culminates in a powerful declaration of readiness for divine alignment, prosperity, leadership, and the fulfillment of covenant blessings, seeking comprehensive restoration across all aspects of life through the power invoked by the blood of Jesus Christ.

30-day Breakthrough Prayer

I. The Petitioner's State and Approach to the Divine

This section details the humble yet determined way the speaker initiates contact with the divine source, acknowledging hardship while relying on a prior invitation.

- The speaker greets the Father with the offering of their "first fruits," symbolizing a dedication of the initial and best resources or efforts.
- A stark acknowledgment of personal condition is made, describing the self as currently "bruised and battled," yet persisting in the approach.
- The very act of coming is predicated on the divine assurance offered to those who are "burdened and heavy laden," seeking the promised rest.
- The petitioner expresses deep gratitude through thanksgiving for the fulfillment of that which is deemed "divine and true."
- A deliberate act of spiritual surrender is performed by laying all personal burdens down "unto and upon your altar."
- This act of submission is intended to compel the fulfillment of divine promises specifically directed toward those who love the Father and are called according to His name.
- The core motivation remains rooted in the recognition of the Father's immense mercy, particularly concerning the afflicted.
- The speaker emphasizes the need for salvation to be bestowed upon the meek, highlighting the soul's desperate cry to the heavens for the prayers to be heard and acknowledged.

II. Urgent Petitions for Deliverance and Family Protection

This theme focuses on the immediate and critical need for divine intervention to rescue loved ones from active threats orchestrated by enemies.

- A swift execution of judgment against adversaries is implored to facilitate the rescue of the speaker's children.
- The severity of the threat is detailed, noting that enemies have formed intricate schemes designed to drag the children "down into the grave."
- A specific grievance is raised regarding grandchildren who have been violently snatched away and subjected to "bondage and wickedness."
- In response to this familial threat, the speaker calls upon the "armies of heaven's angelic host" to intervene actively.
- The angelic mandate includes guarding the endangered family member, ensuring restoration, and protecting her from all forms of harm or danger.
- A specific directive is given for the angels to bring the protected individual back safely to her rightful "own territory."
- The text further describes the enemies' actions as having "plucked her out into an evil place," surrounding her with an environment where iniquity has been deliberately "landscaped."
- The petitioner requests that divine angels be deployed to "lead and hedge" the loved one in defense, ensuring escape from the "wiles of the devil."
- The goal of this protective action is the secure arrival of the loved one into the Father's "safe harbor."

III. Defense Against Personal Malice and Iniquity

This section addresses the direct, unjustified attacks leveled against the speaker, demanding divine protection from those who plot destruction.

- The speaker recognizes the multitude of evil deeds plotted by adversaries, deeds framed as if the speaker were inherently a "destroyer or abomination."

- In contrast to these accusations, the speaker affirms their own role as one who has actively "kept my peace" amidst the turmoil.
- A direct plea for non-judgment or non-surrender is made: "Pass me not onto them that they should eat of my flesh."
- The targeting of the speaker is characterized as being "without just cause."
- The motivation of the attackers is identified as the filling of their own greed through the deployment of "obnoxious terror" and the carrying of "malice to the simple."
- The prayer escalates into a demand for divine counteraction against these evil plots.
- The petitioner calls for the crushing and dividing of the enemies, bringing terror upon them as retribution for their evil attacks.
- A specific spiritual cleansing is demanded: the cancellation of "every Witcher of the four winds of the earth," sending these entities down into the grave they intended for the speaker.
- The speaker demands vengeance and restoration across "every territory where terror lurks to bring destruction."

IV. Comprehensive Spiritual Warfare and Cancellation of Covenants

This theme details the active, verbal renunciation and nullification of all spiritual agreements, monitoring, and demonic influence affecting the speaker's life and destiny.

- The speaker issues a powerful threefold declaration: to "rebuke, cancel and void" any agreement, invitation, or entertainment extended to any "evil host of demonic spirits."
- This cancellation specifically targets familiar spirits and monitoring spirits, declaring their assignments void.

- The speaker assumes the role of the "router" authorized to disengage and cancel these assignments immediately.
- All cords of communication and all points of contact established by these entities are declared "null and void."
- A command is issued for these entities to be ordered into the "abyss of depth into the darkness of the sea," specifically cast into the "hell beneath the sand of the Red Sea."
- The cancellation extends beyond mere spirits to include human agents: "The gangs, cults, criminals, and betrayers" who allied to deceive and destroy the speaker's destiny.
- This cancellation is ratified and sealed "by the blood of Jesus."
- The speaker demands that these adversaries divide their own spoils, forcing them to "eat of their evil deeds that do not belong to me."
- The speaker explicitly rejects any claim upon them regarding wrath, punishment, death, or any demonic energy that might be transmitted, transpired, conspired, or released into their personal spheres.
- This protection covers the entirety of the individual: spirit, body, soul, health, finances, business, ministry, family, home, and environment.

V. Affirmation of Covenant Protection and Divine Favor

Having declared spiritual victory, the focus shifts to affirming the current state of blessedness and requesting the outpouring of established covenant promises.

- A declaration of safety is made: "Calamity is far from me and my loved ones."
- The speaker asserts their belonging to the group of "thy blessed people" who are defended by the Father's "mighty arm."

- The presence of divine protection is affirmed: "Your hand is upon us, with none of them can withstand."
- A request is made for the release of blessings, and the covenant promises upon the speaker.
- The petitioner asks for the heavens to "Pour from the heavens the goodness from your grace."
- This grace is sought to facilitate a transformation in financial standing, specifically to become "the lender and not the borrower."
- Furthermore, the speaker prays that their "seed" (descendants or future endeavors) shall not be forced to "beg of bread."
- Divine favor is sought specifically in influential secular and governmental spheres, including the "courts and council, financial institutions, and policy makers."
- The speaker asks to be covered by this favor throughout "all the days of my life."

VI. Readiness for Prosperity, Leadership, and Strategic Alignment

The final major theme details the desired state of personal transformation, emphasizing productivity, strategic thinking, and the acquisition of divine authority necessary for future dominion.

- The prayer calls for the initiation of "sanctification, restoration, and edification" within the speaker's "temple" (the body/self).
- This internal work is intended to enable movement, productivity, and the capacity to "think strategically."
- The speaker desires to "build with ownership and authority and kingdom privileges."
- These privileges are expected to actively "provoke and ignite health, wealth, prosperity."
- The goal is to bring forth a profound "peace that surpasses understanding," achieved through the glory and the blood of the Lord Jesus Christ.

- Returning to the initial theme of preparation, the speaker requests divine assistance in achieving perfect temporal alignment: readiness, synchronization, and "synchropate my life in divine timing and alignment."
- This alignment must be specifically tethered to purpose and plans designed for success in multiple domains.
- Specific aspirations listed for this aligned state include prosperity in strength, high productivity, effective leadership, and ownership.
- The speaker desires to "build up my gates" (a metaphor for boundaries, influence, or success markers).
- In terms of personal capacity, the request is to excel in "aptitude" and to "soar."
- Finally, the speaker asks for divine empowerment in conflict: "in battle, let me..." (the sentence trails off, implying victory or strength in conflict).

The document, "Great is your mercy," functions as a comprehensive spiritual mandate, moving from humble confession of affliction to aggressive spiritual warfare and culminating in a declaration of intended prosperity and divine alignment. The core takeaway is the petitioner's absolute reliance on the Father's mercy to overcome immediate threats—including familial kidnapping, malicious plotting, and demonic infiltration—by invoking the power of the blood of Jesus to cancel all negative covenants. The prayer establishes a framework where spiritual cleansing directly precedes material and authoritative blessing, ensuring the speaker transitions from being a burdened recipient of grace to an empowered lender, leader, and strategic builder, fully synchronized with divine purpose for health, wealth, and enduring peace. The final appeal emphasizes that this entire process must be witnessed and acknowledged by the highest powers in heaven, confirming the righteousness of the servants who seek these blessings.

30-day Breakthrough Prayer

Chapter 27

Sweet Aroma Prayer

Accept my humble prayer Lord

Create in me a clean heart and renew a right spirit within me

Renew my mind and mental faculties that I articulate according to your righteous and great design, that in all things I honor you for you are in all truth. In faith I believe you have restored my health, I decree and declare my health is restored in fullness, keep my soul in perfect peace in each of my ordered steps direct my path.

Restore unto me the youth of my bones keep and return thy joy unto my soul. I renounce every exalted person, thing and idol that I have served in offense to you. Forgive my foolish heart in placing spirit, anyone or anything human or elemental in thine honor, let thy Holy Spirit be exalted above all.

For you are worthy to be praised and honored and the truth of my salvation. Nothing do I place above or before you, you've kept my place and didn't forget me when I was cast down and mocked by others, you held my hand.

I give my thanks to you I offer my heart, my soul belongs to you. You are the Only righteous one my praise and worship belong to you. On your throne you are exalted, please don't pass me by.

Cast out my enemies, defeat them in my honor because I seek your face with my whole heart. I have tested my trials and give you thanks for delivering me out of deep and troubled waters. The current had overtaken me, the people sought to destroy me for the gift that you gave unto me, for my existence they sought to destroy. War on my behalf Lord Jesus, cover me with your tabernacle, shield me with your wing, direct me with your compass that they cannot reach me. I will not fear mortal men, for you are God. I plead your blood to cover my house, and the home of my children and loved ones.

30-day Breakthrough Prayer

Out of the evil heart of man, they tossed me to and fro, they laughed when I mourned, they spoke evil of my works and cast my property as lots. They took of my inheritance from whence you gave and spoke evil over my children, they took malicious pride in obtaining what I birthed from my womb, and I did mourn. Recompense my own, my value, my worth, my wealth, my loving heart and my youth. Let them eat of their scorn, Father dissolve my tears and remove the pain and misery that was their governance and purpose. In my food and medicine, they placed poison to obtain my life. These evil works I renounce, with the authority of the blood of Jesus I rebuke, cancel and destroy these evil deeds, their intentions and nullify any effects or affliction to cause harm. No weapon formed against me shall prosper. I decree and declare that no weapon formed against me shall prosper, no sickness, death, theft, mourning, devices, images, spells, curses, cancers, blood curses, brooms, witchcraft, sorcery, evil intentions, governance, gang stalking, monitoring spirits, spoken words, hair, voodoo, hoodoo, ancient tombs, satanic alters, rituals, dances, songs nor chants shall prosper against me, in Jesus name, by the blood of Jesus every assignment is canceled. Let vengeance be yours as you have done for your people and those who are called according to your name. Hallelujah, Jehovah Jireh, you are my provider. Reign in your victory, clothe me with peace and prosperity, love, wisdom, joy by your mighty hand. Show me your tender mercies. Abba, father I cry out in a loud voice to the heavens.

Restore my spirit, return my purpose, return my inheritance to me. Perform your miracles on my life, in Jesus's name, my faith belongs to you. You are my wisdom, glory, honor and praise. You sustain my soul.

I am enriched with the Holy Trinity, I am empowered by my God, whose name I call upon in a time of trouble. You have prevailed and victory belongs to you, you have shaken the mountains and given me water from the rocks. You have provided me with overflow and nourishment from the heavens. You have enlarged my territory and restored my life, you brought me honey from the locust, you swallow the bees and no leviathan spirit can defeat you. You have crushed the head of my enemies, and you bring forth the rain. I subdue every one of my enemies, they will humble themselves before my God. Jesus comes to my defense; God has sent his angels to accomplish these works because he delights in me. I give you thanks Jesus as I cast my cares on you. Father God, remove me from the enemy's heart, take their attention to prosper in their ways and not upon me, not upon my destruction, remove them from my heart. Renew and restore my energy into what serves your kingdom and affluent to prosper your people, the building of your kingdom. Show your mercy to your children.

A Comprehensive Exposition of the Sweet Aroma Prayer for Spiritual Restoration and Deliverance

The prayer is characterized by intense declarations of faith, profound requests for spiritual cleansing and renewal, earnest pleas for physical and emotional restoration, and aggressive spiritual warfare aimed at nullifying the works of enemies. It moves sequentially from internal sanctification to external protection, detailing past suffering inflicted by malicious human actions, and culminating in affirmations of divine provision, empowerment through the Holy Trinity, and dedication to building the Kingdom of God. The text serves as both a heartfelt confession of dependence and a powerful decree against all forms of affliction and opposition.

I. Foundations of Spiritual Renewal and Sanctification

This section details the supplicant's initial focus on internal transformation, seeking a state of grace and alignment with divine will.

- The prayer begins with a humble offering, addressing the Lord directly and requesting acceptance of this sincere petition.

- A core request is the creation of a "clean heart," signifying a desire for moral purity and freedom from hidden sin or defilement.
- The supplicant asks for the renewal of a "right spirit within," emphasizing the need for an internal disposition that is aligned with righteousness and truth.
- The petition extends to the renewal of the mind and mental faculties, seeking transformation so that all articulation and thought processes conform to God's "righteous and great design."
- There is a commitment expressed to honor God in all aspects of life, acknowledging His ultimate truthfulness and sovereignty over all matters.
- This foundational request establishes the internal state necessary before addressing external battles or seeking physical restoration.

II. Declarations of Faith in Health, Peace, and Joy

This theme focuses on actively decreeing positive outcomes based on existing faith, moving from passive request to active declaration.

- The supplicant declares, in faith, the belief that health has already been restored by the Lord.
- This belief is solidified through decree and declaration, asserting that health is restored "in fullness," leaving no room for doubt regarding physical well-being.
- A specific request is made for the soul to be kept in "perfect peace," ensuring tranquility regardless of external circumstances.
- The prayer asks for divine guidance in every "ordered step," seeking direction and purpose in the daily path forward.
- A powerful petition is made for physical rejuvenation, asking the Lord to "Restore unto me the youth of my bones."
- Crucially, the return of spiritual vitality is sought through the request to "keep and return thy

joy unto my soul," indicating a prior state of diminished joy.

III. Renunciation of Idolatry and Exaltation of the Holy Spirit

This segment addresses spiritual allegiance, ensuring that the focus of worship remains solely on the divine.

- The supplicant actively renounces every "exalted person, thing and idol" that has been served, acknowledging these as offenses against the Lord.
- Forgiveness is sought for the "foolish heart" that mistakenly placed any spirit, human entity, or elemental force in the position of honor due only to God.
- The central focus of this section is the explicit exaltation of the Holy Spirit, demanding that the Spirit be elevated "above all" other influences or powers.
- The worthiness of the Lord to be praised and honored is affirmed, linking this worship directly to the truth of the supplicant's salvation.
- A declaration of ultimate priority is made: "Nothing do I place above or before you," reinforcing singular devotion.
- Gratitude is expressed for God's faithfulness, noting that the Lord maintained the supplicant's place and did not forget them during times of being cast down and mocked by others, emphasizing divine support ("you held my hand").

IV. Offering of Self and Plea for Divine Presence

This theme centers on total surrender and the recognition of God's unique position as the righteous one.

- The supplicant offers complete gratitude, presenting their heart as a gift, and declaring that their soul belongs entirely to the Lord.

- The recognition of God as the "Only righteous one" is stated, establishing the basis for all praise and worship directed toward Him.
- A direct plea is made for divine attention and intervention: "On your throne you are exalted, please don't pass me by."
- The prayer shifts to a request for active intervention against adversaries, asking that enemies be cast out and defeated "in my honor" because the supplicant seeks God's face with their whole heart.
- Thanks are given for past deliverances, specifically mentioning being rescued from "deep and troubled waters" where the current had overtaken them.
- The intensity of the opposition is highlighted: people sought to destroy the supplicant specifically because of the "gift" bestowed upon them, leading to attempts to destroy their very existence.

V. Warfare, Protection, and Sanctification of Home

This section moves into explicit spiritual warfare, requesting divine shielding and the application of redemptive power over the household.

- The supplicant calls upon "Lord Jesus" to wage war on their behalf.
- A request for comprehensive divine covering is made: to be covered with the Lord's "tabernacle" and shielded with His "wing."
- Guidance is sought through God's "compass" so that enemies cannot reach the supplicant.
- A declaration of fearlessness is made: "I will not fear mortal men, for you are God."
- A critical protective measure is invoked: pleading the blood of Jesus to cover the supplicant's house, the homes of their children, and the homes of loved ones.
- This section establishes a boundary of divine protection around the entire family unit.

VI. Lamentation Over Malicious Acts and Theft

This part of the prayer details the specific, painful injustices suffered at the hands of others, providing context for the subsequent requests for recompense and nullification.

- The supplicant describes being tossed to and fro due to the "evil heart of man."
- The cruelty of the oppressors is detailed: they laughed during the supplicant's mourning.
- The enemies spoke evil of the supplicant's works and treated their property as spoils, casting lots for possessions.
- A significant grievance is the theft of inheritance—that which the Lord had originally given—followed by the speaking of evil curses over the supplicant's children.
- The suffering extended to personal loss and grief, including mourning over "malicious pride in obtaining what I birthed from my womb."
- The pain involved the loss of personal value, worth, wealth, loving heart, and youth, which the enemies unjustly claimed.
- The depth of the attack is revealed through the accusation that poison was placed in the supplicant's food and medicine to steal their life.

VII. Comprehensive Renunciation and Nullification of Evil Assignments

This is the most detailed section regarding spiritual warfare, where specific curses and attacks are named and forcefully rejected through the authority of Jesus' blood.

- The supplicant formally renounces all the "evil works" mentioned previously.
- With the authority derived from the blood of Jesus, the supplicant rebukes, cancels, and

destroys these evil deeds, their intentions, and nullifies any resulting affliction or harm.

- A powerful, repeated decree is issued: "No weapon formed against me shall prosper."
- This decree is then itemized, listing every conceivable form of attack that is declared ineffective: sickness, death, theft, mourning, devices, images, spells, curses, cancers, blood curses, brooms, witchcraft, sorcery, evil intentions, governance, gang stalking, monitoring spirits, spoken words, hair, voodoo, hoodoo, ancient tombs, satanic alters, rituals, dances, songs, nor chants.
- The prayer asserts that by the blood of Jesus, "every assignment is canceled."
- The supplicant then delegates vengeance to the Lord, asking that divine retribution be executed upon those who have acted against God's people.
- The prayer shifts to affirmation, praising Jehovah Jireh as the provider and requesting that the Lord reign in victory.
- The supplicant asks to be clothed by God's hand with peace, prosperity, love, wisdom, and joy.
- The section concludes with a desperate, loud cry to the heavens, addressing God as "Abba, father."

VIII. Restoration of Self, Purpose, and Inheritance

Having declared spiritual warfare and renunciation, the focus returns to reclaiming what was lost and affirming divine empowerment.

- Specific items requested for restoration include the spirit, purpose, and inheritance.
- The supplicant asks the Lord to "Perform your miracles on my life," grounding this request in the faith that belongs to Jesus.
- God is acknowledged as the source of wisdom, glory, honor, and praise, and the sustainer of the soul.

- The supplicant affirms a state of being "enriched with the Holy Trinity" and empowered by God, whose name is called upon in times of trouble.
- The Lord is praised for enlarging the supplicant's territory and restoring life, bringing forth sustenance metaphorically described as "honey from the locust."
- The power of God is affirmed over spiritual opposition, noting that no "leviathan spirit can defeat you."
- The crushing of the enemies' heads is declared, and the supplicant asserts their ability to subdue every enemy, forcing them to humble themselves before God.
- Divine defense is acknowledged: Jesus comes to the defense, and God sends angels because He "delights in me."
- The supplicant casts their cares upon Jesus and thanks Him.

IX. Final Requests for Redirection and Mercy

The concluding segment focuses on psychological release from the oppressors and redirecting personal energy toward constructive, kingdom-focused endeavors.

- A plea is made to the Father God to remove the supplicant from the enemy's heart and mind.
- The request is that the enemies focus their attention on prospering in their own ways, rather than focusing on the supplicant's destruction.
- The supplicant asks for the enemies to be removed from their own heart, signifying a desire to release bitterness or obsession with the conflict.
- A crucial request for energy renewal follows: the supplicant asks for their energy to be restored specifically into activities that "serves your kingdom."
- This energy must be affluent and dedicated to prospering God's people and the "building of your kingdom."

- The prayer concludes with a final, tender appeal for divine compassion: "Show your mercy to your children."

The "Sweet Aroma Prayer" is a comprehensive spiritual document that maps the journey from deep personal affliction to triumphant declaration of faith. It systematically addresses the need for internal purification (clean heart, renewed mind) before engaging in external conflict. The text functions as a powerful legal appeal, where past injustices—including theft, slander, and attempts on life through poisoning—are laid before the court of heaven. The core takeaway is the absolute reliance on the authority of Jesus' blood to nullify every conceivable spiritual attack, ranging from witchcraft and curses to organized stalking and monitoring spirits. Furthermore, the prayer is not solely focused on defense; it is equally dedicated to restoration—of health, youth, purpose, and inheritance—and culminates in a commitment to redirect all renewed strength toward serving the divine kingdom and showing mercy to fellow believers. The document stands as a testament to enduring faith amidst severe persecution, demanding divine intervention, protection for the family, and ultimate victory through God's power.

30-day Breakthrough Prayer

Chapter 29

Fervent Prayer

James 5:16

" Confess your faults one to another, and pray one for another, that ye may be healed. The effectual fervent prayer of a righteous man availeth much."

Today, I set forth my declaration's, and I decree my prayer life is activated into the Heavenly realm and will not just remain earthbound. Today, I am renewed. What I release into the heavens God will hear and answer me. I establish my faith and destiny to be prosperous, effective and productive in my life and all my endeavors, purpose and needs are fulfilled. I decree and declare that my health, mental, physical and spiritual life are in wellness and good order, my family's needs are improved and functioning in divine order and my purpose is in accordance to the goodness of God, my business and financial needs are being met with increase and unexpected influx, surplus, my church and social life is healthy, positive and God surrounds the people, places and opportunities to serve me for my good. I place God the Father, Son and Holy Spirit at the head of my life, that he will defend and cover me; no weapon formed against me shall prosper. I am more than a conqueror through Christ Jesus who continues to strengthen me. He has sat me in my rightful place of authority to operate dominion upon the earth. I am blessed and I release the battle unto the Lord. I am free, in the name of Jesus Christ.

Running The Race, the baton is in your hand. Run for your life. Trust God, in God we trust! Be not confused with who and where your God is, you got to know his address. 1 Cor. 6:19 what? "No, you not that your body is the temple of the Holy Ghost, which is in you, which you have of God, and you are not your own." (Our bodies are the temple of God).

Keep awareness of where He is always, seeking what He requires of you. Be studious and steadfast in what you are competing for. This competition has already been won for us, when Christ died on the cross. The question is can you keep the winning cup without turning it over into the hands of this "Satan" the world.

Run the race for your life. Hebrews 12:1-3 Therefore, since we are surrounded by such a great cloud of witnesses, let us throw off everything that hinders and the sin that so easily entangles. And let us run with perseverance the race marked out for us,[2] fixing our eyes on Jesus, the pioneer and perfecter of faith. For the joy set before him he endured the cross, scorning its shame, and sat down at the right hand of the throne of God. [3] Consider him who endured such opposition from sinners, so that you will not grow weary and lose heart.

When we run without conditioning, we tire fast, get leg cramps, out of breath and most of us aren't prepared to run the distance. Some may be more conditioned than others, because of natural exercise and fitness. But for this teaching, our conditioning is the word of God, not a track field. But our minds and habits must be in condition to be prepared for the spiritual competition that we are up against. We have been selected or have been chosen to compete when we decide Christ as our Lord and savior because we as good stewards understand that the enemy is to distract us or turn us away from our high calling.

The enemy comes to steal, kill and destroy our high calling. He brings his best game to place us in a marathon, more than any relay. The enemy's objective is that we lose at all costs. His position is opposition, adversity, controversy, contradiction, addiction, distraction and destruction. There's a whole list of what he won't stop at doing to make us lose. I've been to rock bottom, fallen in the race and I'm sure my Heavenly Father was disappointed. Luckily Gods will be for us to win, he forgives us and already knows our shortcomings to overcome evil, overcome darkness, become disciplined and prepared for our battles to make it to the holy gates. His desire is that he can tell us in the end, well done. There is a song that says, "I just want to make it to heaven and hear him say well done." that song touches my heart, I want to hear those words.

Running for anything against an opponent is never an easy task, look at how low politicians go to win an election, most lie and will cheat. Well, the one we are running against is tricky, clever, will lie and have you disqualified so we prepare ourselves for the battle, and take the assignment seriously because it is our destiny, our lives, our children lives because he doesn't just come after us, but our bloodline as well.

In a busy life with all the demands and challenges we face, some of us feel we don't have time to pray or lack the discipline for consistency. These two things are requisite for preparation. Anybody have difficulty fasting? Pray without ceasing Ephesians 6:18 Amplified "With all prayer and petition pray [with specific requests] at all times [on every occasion and in every season] in the Spirit, and with this in view, stay alert with all perseverance and petition [interceding in prayer] for all God's people."

Running for Jesus is not easy but as it is written in Philippians 3:14 I press toward the mark for the prize of the high calling of God in Christ Jesus.

Has anybody ever been to hell and back? I think I may have ran right into hell. How do you get out of a situation like that? Sometimes even repeated cycles because we don't start out with discipline, but rather chastisement.

30-day Breakthrough Prayer

Hebrews 12:6-11 KJV

6 For whom the Lord love he chasten and scourge
every son whom he receives.

7 If ye endure chastening, God deal with you as with
sons; for what son is he whom the father chastens
not?

8 But if ye be without chastisement, whereof all are
partakers, then are ye bastards, and not sons.

9 Furthermore we have had fathers of our flesh which
corrected us, and we gave them reverence: shall we
not much rather be in subjection unto the Father of
spirits, and live?

10 For they verily for a few days chastened us after
their own pleasure; but he for our profit, that we
might be partakers of his holiness.

11 Now no chastening for the present seems to be
joyous, but grievous: nevertheless, afterward it
yields the peaceable fruit of righteousness unto
them which are exercised thereby. Hallelujah to the
word and reading of scripture.

After going through the lessons of discipline, some people get bitter or angry with God or confused on rather it was a beaten from the Devil or the discipline of God. The difference between the two, is God loves his children, and is working to refrain you from the direction you are headed. Satan, on the other hand simply want to destroy your life. You'll know the difference because I have yet to hear Satan ever saved a child of God.

The rewards of staying in the race is the ability to gain eternal life, a blessed life that is refined. Many blessings God has written for his children to be heirs. Have an Inheritance. Free from torment, to overcome evil. The greatest gift, which is love, something we all need to share.

When it was all said and done, who was stood with me? Who pulled me away, who never left when I wanted to give up, who loved me more than I loved myself, why am I here to testify, why I am still in the race? Thanks! and glory to the Lord Jesus Christ.

The Spiritual Marathon: Perseverance, Conditioning, and the High Calling in Christ

This document serves as an intensive exhortation and teaching centered on the Christian life viewed through the metaphor of running a demanding race. It emphasizes the urgency of running "for your life," stressing that the spiritual competition requires absolute focus, proper conditioning through the Word of God, and unwavering perseverance. The text outlines the nature of the victory already secured by Christ, the constant threat posed by the adversary ("Satan" or "the world"), and the necessary spiritual disciplines—prayer and fasting—required to maintain the course. Furthermore, it delves into the critical distinction between divine discipline (chastisement for profit and holiness) and the destructive intent of the enemy, ultimately focusing on the rewards of enduring to the end, culminating in hearing the affirmation, "well done."

The Mandate to Run and Establishing Identity

- The fundamental instruction is to "Run The Race," recognizing that the baton is now in the runner's hand, demanding a life lived with urgency.
- Trust in God is paramount, requiring believers to know precisely "who and where your God is," establishing a clear spiritual address.
- This identity is rooted in the understanding derived from 1 Corinthians 6:19: the body is the temple of the Holy Ghost, residing within the believer, signifying that the individual does not belong to themselves but to God. This realization underpins the seriousness of the competition.

- Believers must maintain constant awareness of God's presence and diligently seek His requirements, maintaining studiousness and steadfastness regarding the goal of the competition.

The Secured Victory and the Present Challenge

- The document firmly establishes that the ultimate competition—the victory over sin and death—has already been decisively won through the crucifixion of Christ on the cross.
- The current spiritual challenge is not about winning the initial battle, but rather about maintaining that victory, specifically questioning whether the believer can "keep the winning cup without turning it over into the hands of this 'Satan' the world."
- The race must be run for one's life, drawing heavily upon the exhortation found in Hebrews 12:1-3, which serves as the foundational text for perseverance.

Principles of Perseverance Drawn from Scripture (Hebrews 12:1-3)

- To successfully navigate the race, believers are instructed to actively "throw off everything that hinders and the sin that so easily entangles." This requires intentional removal of obstacles.
- The focus must remain fixed: runners must keep their "eyes on Jesus," who is identified as both the pioneer and the perfecter of faith.
- Jesus serves as the ultimate example of endurance, having endured the cross and its accompanying shame for the joy set before Him, ultimately sitting down at the right hand of the throne of God.
- Believers are encouraged to constantly "Consider him who endured such opposition from sinners" as a direct means to prevent themselves from growing weary and losing heart during their own trials.

Spiritual Conditioning vs. Physical Fitness

- The text draws a clear analogy between physical running and spiritual competition, noting that running without conditioning leads to predictable failures: fatigue, cramps, breathlessness, and an inability to complete the distance.
- While acknowledging that some individuals may possess natural advantages ("natural exercise and fitness"), the document clarifies that for spiritual teaching, the required conditioning is not derived from a track field.
- The true conditioning agent is identified as "the word of God."
- The minds and habits of the competitors must be rigorously conditioned to prepare them for the spiritual competition they face.
- The act of choosing Christ as Lord and Savior is framed as the moment of selection or being chosen to compete, understanding that the enemy's primary objective is to distract or divert the believer from this "high calling."

The Nature and Tactics of the Enemy

- The enemy's overarching objective is destructive: to "steal, kill and destroy our high calling."
- The adversary approaches this task with maximum effort, treating the believer's journey as a marathon rather than a relay, indicating a sustained, long-term assault.
- The enemy's singular objective is ensuring the believer loses "at all costs."
- The enemy's arsenal of tactics is extensive and multifaceted, listed specifically as: opposition, adversity, controversy, contradiction, addiction, distraction, and destruction. The text notes there is "a whole list" of actions the enemy will undertake.
- The scope of the enemy's attack is broad, extending beyond the individual believer to encompass the entire "bloodline."

30-day Breakthrough Prayer

Confronting Failure, Receiving Forgiveness, and Maintaining Desire

- The author shares a personal testimony of failure, admitting to having reached "rock bottom" and fallen in the race, acknowledging the potential disappointment of the Heavenly Father.
- Despite such failings, the document emphasizes the grace available: God's will be for believers to win, He forgives shortcomings, and He already knows these weaknesses, preparing the believer to overcome evil and darkness.
- The ultimate desire articulated is to successfully complete the journey and hear God say, "well done," a sentiment that deeply touches the author's heart.

The Seriousness of the Assignment and Requisite Preparation

- Running against an opponent is inherently difficult, drawing parallels to the low tactics employed by politicians seeking election, such as lying and cheating.
- The spiritual opponent is particularly "tricky, clever," and willing to lie to achieve disqualification.
- Therefore, preparation must be serious because the stakes involve destiny, individual lives, and the lives of future generations (the bloodline).
- In the context of a busy life filled with demands, two specific spiritual disciplines are identified as requisite for preparation: prayer and fasting.
- A lack of time or discipline for consistency in these areas is a common struggle.
- Scriptural guidance for prayer is provided via Ephesians 6: 18 (Amplified), commanding believers to "Pray without ceasing," engaging in prayer and petition with specific requests "at all times [on every occasion and in every season] in the Spirit," maintaining alertness with perseverance and petition on behalf of all God's people.

Pressing Toward the Mark

- The difficulty of running for Jesus is acknowledged, but this difficulty is contextualized by the goal stated in Philippians 3:14: to "press toward the mark for the prize of the high calling of God in Christ Jesus."
- The text briefly touches upon extreme spiritual distress, referencing experiences akin to running "right into hell," and questions how one escapes such cycles, suggesting that escape often requires moving beyond mere chastisement toward true discipline.

Understanding Divine Discipline (Hebrews 12:6-11 KJV)

- The document transitions to a detailed exposition of Hebrews 12:6-11 (KJV) to clarify the nature of trials and correction.
- The Lord chastens and scourges every son whom He receives, implying that enduring chastening is evidence of sonship.
- Those who are exempt from chastisement are categorized as "bastards, and not sons."
- Believers are urged to submit to the Father of spirits, just as they submitted to earthly fathers who corrected them, to live.
- Earthly fathers corrected for a few days as they pleased, but God corrects for the believer's ultimate profit, ensuring they become "partakers of his holiness."
- While chastening may not seem joyous but grievous in the present, it ultimately yields "the peaceable fruit of righteousness" for those who are exercised by it.

Distinguishing God's Discipline from Satanic Attack

- Following the scriptural lesson on discipline, the text addresses potential confusion: some believers become bitter, angry, or confused, unable to discern whether a trial is a "beaten from the Devil or the discipline of God."

- The fundamental difference lies in motivation: God loves His children and seeks to restrain them from a destructive path.
- Satan, conversely, "simply want to destroy your life."
- The definitive test for identification is provided: the author has never heard of Satan saving a child of God, whereas God's action always involves salvation and restoration.

The Rewards of Staying in the Race

- The rewards for successfully remaining in the race are substantial and eternal.
- These include gaining eternal life and achieving a "blessed life that is refined."
- Believers are promised an Inheritance, as God has written many blessings for His children to be heirs.
- Further rewards include being "Free from torment, to overcome evil."
- The greatest gift highlighted, which all runners need to share, is love.

Final Testimony and Gratitude

- The teaching concludes with a reflective moment, asking who stood with the runner when everything else failed.
- The author testifies to the presence of the one who pulled them away from giving up, who loved them more than they loved themselves, and who remains the reason for their current testimony and continued participation in the race.
- The final acknowledgment is one of profound gratitude: "Thanks and glory to the Lord Jesus Christ."

The prayer powerfully asserts that the Christian journey is an active, demanding race requiring immediate commitment and lifelong perseverance. Victory over sin is already achieved through Christ, but the daily execution of faith demands rigorous spiritual conditioning rooted in the Word of God, constant vigilance against the enemy's tactics of distraction and destruction, and unwavering focus on Jesus as the model of endurance. Preparation hinges on the non-negotiable disciplines of prayer and fasting. Crucially, believers must correctly interpret hardship, understanding that divine chastisement is a loving mechanism for achieving holiness and righteousness, distinct from the destructive intent of the adversary. The ultimate motivation for enduring this difficult marathon is the promise of eternal life, a refined existence, and the profound reward of hearing God's final affirmation of approval.

Chapter 29

You Are Great Beyond Greatness

Greater is He who lives in me than he that lives in the world. Great is your mercy towards me. Make fresh my anointing that I shall be quickened and come to life. Deliver me from what brings lethal and vital harm to me in this spirit, body, mind and so that my soul is recompensed from death and destruction. I realize that my blessings come from you oh God, precious are your children in your sight. I realize that my deliverance comes from you, and not something that I could achieve on my own. I realize that my greatness comes from you, and for what you have created in me I give you thanks, honor, and praise. I believe and put My Hope in you, that you will continue to do great things in my life. You have provided me with great vision, and I thank you for the sight and all abilities that you bestowed upon me.

Many troubles I have experienced before and through the vision, I delight in every trial which has given me assurity of all things being made possible through your mighty strength, for all who Love the Lord, and are called according to His purpose. You have sustained my weakness and given great strength, you have given me great power and strength to press for the higher calling; therefore, in whatever I do I will prevail and offer great service to others.

Your greatness reaches the highest mountains, let my greatness be used to glorify your name and let me be characterized according to your name. Place me into the surplus of your blessings as you do a new thing in the newness of life restoration in me. In your word, you said the first will be last and the last will be first, let this season be the season of blessings and favor as my stature of character reflect the miracles of your great work, and the sufficiency of your grace.

I ask merciful of your favor and that my steps are ordered that I shall not stumble or fall, but be rooted in perpetual purpose, leadership and obedience. By your word, I have been placed as the head and not the tail, and before the foundations of the earth, you knew me, you numbered the hairs on my head and formed me in the womb of my mother. Let no evil or unrighteousness devour my purpose, the purpose you have and desire for me. Let no false identities or theft of my identity or plagiarism to my existence prosper. Canopy your angels and protection around my camp, children, and make my hands and mental fruitful to achieve great works. Create in me a clean heart and renew a right spirit within. Sustain my rightful place according to your kingdom. My honor is in reverence to your greatness and mercy. Many sins have you forgiven, you accept those broken in spirit and heart and bring it to pass. You take the broken and make whole, in all things I give you thanks.

Let thy seed prosper, protect my children and direct each of them with time orchestrated sequence to be protected, productive and blessed.

30-day Breakthrough Prayer

A Declaration of Divine Reliance and Transcendent Greatness

This document serves as a profound spiritual declaration centered on the theme that the divine presence residing within the believer is superior to any worldly power ("Greater is He who lives in me than he that lives in the world"). It is a comprehensive expression of faith, acknowledging that all blessings, deliverance, strength, and purpose originate solely from God. The text moves through stages of petition, thanksgiving, and commitment, requesting divine intervention for protection against harm, guidance in daily steps, restoration of spirit, and the fulfillment of a predestined purpose. It emphasizes a life characterized by service, obedience, and the reflection of God's miraculous work through the believer's transformed character, culminating in a plea for the prosperity and protection of future generations.

The Supremacy of the Divine Presence and Mercy

This section details the foundational belief in the overwhelming power of the Holy Spirit compared to external forces, coupled with an acknowledgment of profound divine mercy.

- The core affirmation is established: The power of the entity residing within the believer surpasses that which resides in the world, establishing a hierarchy of spiritual authority.
- A fervent request is made for the renewal and revitalization of the believer's anointing, seeking immediate spiritual quickening and a return to vibrant life.
- A critical plea for deliverance is issued, targeting anything that poses lethal or vital harm to the believer across all dimensions of existence.
- Protection is sought for the physical body, safeguarding it from elements that threaten its well-being and function.

- The goal of this deliverance is articulated: that the soul may be fully recompensed, recovering from the threat of death and the consequences of destruction.

Acknowledgment of Divine Origin for Greatness and Deliverance

This theme focuses on the explicit recognition that personal achievements, deliverance, and inherent greatness are gifts, not self-attained accomplishments.

- The believer explicitly acknowledges that deliverance is an act originating from God, not a result of personal capability or independent effort.
- A parallel recognition is made regarding personal greatness: it is understood to be derived entirely from the divine source, not from self-generated power.
- There is a firm declaration of faith and hope placed entirely in God, trusting that He will continue to manifest great and significant works within the believer's life trajectory.

Petition for Divine Ordering, Purpose, and Protection

This part of the declaration focuses on specific requests for God to order the believer's path, secure their identity, and surround them with protective forces.

- A humble request is made for the continuation of merciful favor to guide the believer's daily existence.
- A specific petition is offered that the believer's steps be divinely ordered, ensuring they do not stumble or fall in their journey.
- This ordered path must result in the believer being firmly rooted in perpetual purpose, demonstrating unwavering leadership qualities, and maintaining strict obedience.

- The believer affirms a divinely ordained position based on scripture: being placed as the head and not relegated to the position of the tail.
- A profound theological statement is made regarding predestination: that before the foundations of the earth were laid, the believer was known by God.
- The intimate level of divine knowledge is highlighted through the reference to the numbering of every hair on the head.
- The formation process within the mother's womb is cited as evidence of God's deliberate, formative action.
- A strong intercessory request is made to prevent any evil or unrighteous influence from consuming or devouring the divinely appointed purpose.
- A protective barrier is requested against any form of false identity being imposed upon the believer.
- Protection is sought against the theft or plagiarism of one's existence or destiny, ensuring that the unique purpose remains inviolate.
- A call is made for the canopy of angels and divine protection to surround the believer's camp, signifying comprehensive security.
- This protection is extended specifically to the believer's children, ensuring their safety within the divine sphere of influence.
- A request is made for the believer's hands and mental faculties to be made fruitful, enabling the achievement of great works.
- A plea for internal spiritual renewal is voiced: the creation of a clean heart and the restoration of a right spirit within the innermost being.
- The believer seeks divine intervention to sustain their rightful place and standing within the framework of God's kingdom.
- The believer’s honor is defined not by worldly standards but by a deep reverence for God's greatness and enduring mercy.

The final area addresses the need for transformation, the manifestation of God's work through character, and provision for the next generation.

30-day Breakthrough Prayer

- The document acknowledges the multitude of sins that have been forgiven by God, recognizing the depth of divine pardon.
- It affirms God's nature to accept those who are broken in spirit and heart, bringing their difficult circumstances to fruition.
- A powerful statement of divine restorative capability is made God takes what is broken and makes it whole in all aspects of life.
- For all these acts of restoration and forgiveness, the believer offers continuous thanks.
- The believer declares that their greatness must be utilized specifically to glorify the name of God, making divine renown the primary objective.
- A desire is expressed to be characterized in a manner that directly reflects the nature and attributes of God's name.
- A petition is made to be placed into the surplus or abundance of divine blessings.
- This influx of blessing is tied to the concept of God doing a "new thing" within the believer, initiating a process of life restoration.
- The believer invokes the scriptural promise that the first shall become the last, and the last shall become the first, applying this principle to their current season.
- The current season is specifically designated as a season of blessings and divine favor.
- The desired outcome of this season is that the believer's stature of character will visibly reflect the miracles accomplished by God's great work.
- The sufficiency of God's grace is recognized as the underlying foundation that supports this transformation and character development.
- A specific plea is made regarding the believer's seed (offspring), asking that their seed be caused to prosper according to divine will.
- The believer requests divine protection specifically for their children.

- Furthermore, a request is made for God to direct each child according to a time-orchestrated sequence.
- The ultimate state sought for the children is that they be protected, productive in their endeavors, and ultimately blessed by divine favor.
- This entire declaration serves as a comprehensive commitment to live a life wholly dependent upon, and reflective of, the greatness that resides within.

The document "You are Greater beyond Greatness" functions as an intensive spiritual covenant, meticulously detailing the believer's absolute reliance on the divine power inherent within them. The key takeaways revolve around the supremacy of the indwelling God over all worldly challenges, the necessity of acknowledging God as the sole source of deliverance, strength, and vision, and the commitment to endure trials as pathways to greater power. The text moves beyond personal salvation to encompass a holistic request for divine ordering of all steps, robust protection against spiritual and existential threats, and the internal renewal required to manifest a clean heart and right spirit. Ultimately, the declaration culminates in a profound desire for character transformation that mirrors divine attributes, ensuring that all blessings received are leveraged for God's glory, and extends this hope for prosperity, protection, and divinely orchestrated success to future generations. The overarching message is one of complete surrender and faith in a God whose greatness guarantees victory and restoration in every aspect of life.

30-day Breakthrough Prayer

Chapter 30

Image of God

Heavenly Father,

I come before you with thanksgiving for all that you have been and all that you are, I thank you for who you have created me to be. I thank you for who you are creating me to become. I thank you for all things. I thank you for having made me in your image, that I know that who I am, you are also. I asked that you do a perfect work in me, continue to build me , remove the things that is in me that ought not, restore me where I have been broken, rebuild and heal me, remove sickness mental, physical, and spiritual weaknesses , addictions, poverty , idleness, confusion, disorganization, pain, regret, guilt, shame, resentment, anger, past failures, chaos, idolatry, falsehoods. I humbly come before You, acknowledging and reflecting upon my identity as being created in Your divine image, rebuild and restore my body, mind and Spirit. Allow me to operate within my inherent worth and the unique reflection of Your nature within me. I have been carefully crafted with intention, with a divine purpose and essence that calls me into relationship with You.

Lord, engage me in this prayer and reflection, i recognize how essential it is to know you, and I cast my cares on you. I also understand your ways are not my ways, and my ways are not your ways, let your ways shape and make form in my life. Help me to be more like you. You are holy. I seek your love, grace, and mercy.

Father, we acknowledge the struggles we face in the world in pursuit of this divine image. In Romans 8:29, Your Word reminds me that I am "predestined to be conformed to the image of his Son." Yet, I find myself falling short of this calling. Forgive me my shortcomings, align my purpose with the purpose you have for me. I seek transformation of my heart, that my thoughts, words, and actions might mirror the character of Christ. Grant me the strength to surrender myself entirety to Your will.

In my quest to be more like You, Lord, I seek to cultivate virtues that reflect Your nature. Galatians 5:22-23 I speak of the fruits of the Spirit: love, joy, peace, forbearance, kindness, goodness, faithfulness, gentleness, and self-control. May these fruits flourish in my life, enabling me to act as the temple of God in my life, that this reflection may also be an example in the world.

I ask for Your guidance in deepening my relationship with You. In 2 Corinthians 3:18, I am assured that "we all, who with unveiled faces contemplate the Lord's glory, are being transformed into his image with ever-increasing glory." May my prayer be fervently effective. In Jesus name.

Amen.

As we conclude this 30 Days Breakthrough Prayer Guide, it is imperative to reflect upon a profound truth that permeates our understanding of prayer, purpose, and our identity as believers: the idea that humankind is created in the image of God. This foundational concept serves not only as a reminder of our divine origin but also as an invitation to engage with our Creator in a transformative relationship.

Genesis 1:26-27 states, "Then God said, 'Let us make man in our image, after our likeness.' So God created man in his own image, in the image of God he created him; male and female he created them." This initial declaration establishes the dignity, worth, and responsibility endowed upon humanity. Being created in God's image means that we are imbued with qualities that reflect His nature—rationality, creativity, and the capacity for relationship, among others. It invites us to act as His representatives on earth, tasked with stewarding His creation and embodying His character. As we have engaged in prayer over the past 30 days, we have been trained not merely to seek provisions but to embody the virtues of our Creator, fostering within us the understanding that prayer is a dialogue with the One whose image we bear.

Moreover, this understanding of the "Image of God" reinforces our need for community. In Genesis 2:18, it is stated, "The Lord God said, 'It is not good that the man should be alone; I will make him a helper fit for him.'" This indicates that even within the divine image, there exists a pattern of relationality. Our walk with God is not meant to be solitary; we are designed to exist in community, both with Him and with each other. As we prayed for breakthroughs, healing, and clarity over the last month, we were also reminded of the need to support one another as God's image-bearers, reflecting His love and grace in our interactions. The prayers we lifted were not solely for ourselves, but rather an extension of our relational mandate—acting in a way that echoes God's love and compassion.

Additionally, the New Testament reinforces this identity in numerous ways. In Ephesians 4:24, Paul encourages us to "put on the new self, created after the likeness of God in true righteousness and holiness." This call to authenticity and transformation is rooted in our identity as God's creation. Here, we see that being made in His image is an ongoing journey. Our prayers during this season have focused on areas where we seek breakthroughs, healing, and renewal. We must recognize that God's transformative power is at work within us, turning us continually into the likeness of Christ, who is the perfect image of God (Colossians 1:15).

Moreover, the essence of our prayer life is fundamentally tied to His image within us. The writer of Hebrews reminds us in Hebrews 4:16, "Let us then with confidence draw near to the throne of grace, that we may receive mercy and find grace to help in time of need." Our privilege to approach God in prayer rests on the assurance that we are made in His image and that He desires a relationship with us. As we prayed daily, we did so with the knowledge that we are seen, heard, and valued—not just as servants, but as beloved children created in His image. This inviolable truth shapes our prayers, igniting a passion that yearns for more than mere requests; we crave a deeper communion with our Creator.

Lastly, we bear witness to the ultimate fulfillment of our identity in God through Jesus Christ. In 1 John 3:2, we find profound encouragement: "Beloved, we are God's children now, and what we will has not yet appeared; but we know that when he appears we shall be like him, because we shall see him as he is." This hope is the heartbeat of our faith that calls us to understand that our identity as bearers of God's image is not static but progressive. Each prayer, each breakthrough, catapults us into deeper expressions of His glory and character, reminding us of the future hope we hold—a glorious transformation into His likeness.

As you close this guide, let the essence of being created in the image of God resonate profoundly within you. Your prayers may have sought breakthroughs, but they have also unearthed the reality of your identity as an image of God. May we live in the awareness of this divine truth, emboldened in our prayers and actions to reflect His glory into the world around us. May each prayer result not only in fulfillment but in a powerful affirmation of our longing to walk as true children of God, created in His image. Let us continue to engage in this ministry of reconciliation, praying for one another, and reminding ourselves that we serve a God who desires intimacy with His creation. In doing so, we step into the fullness of life and purpose that He has ordained us from the beginning.

Sew a Seed!

All proceeds from the 30-Day Breakthrough will serve as a seed of hope, benefiting the Purple Monday Foundation to support both faith-based and community initiatives. To aid us in this ministry and enable us to provide more teachings and materials like this, consider making a pledge to the Purple Monday Organization for Empowerment. Your contribution will help us share messages of hope and valuable resources.

- **Website:** www.purplemondayfoundation.org
- **Email:** purplemonday.org@gmail.com

Thank you!

Stay prayed up!

www.ingramcontent.com/pod-product-compliance
Lightning Source LLC
LaVergne TN
LVHW020709110826
845149LV00012B/2178